MAC
&
CHEESE

To Jeremy Kingery, the Mac to my Cheese.

When using kitchen appliances please always follow the manufacturer's instructions.

HQ
An imprint of HarperCollins*Publishers* Ltd
1 London Bridge Street
London SE1 9GF

www.harpercollins.co.uk

HarperCollins*Publishers*
Macken House
39/40 Mayor Street Upper
Dublin 1
D01 C9W8
Ireland

10 9 8 7 6 5 4 3

First published in Great Britain by
HQ, an imprint of HarperCollins*Publishers* Ltd 2023

A catalogue record for this book is available from the British Library.

ISBN: 978-0-00-865223-4

MIX
Paper | Supporting responsible forestry
FSC™ C007454

This book contains FSC™ certified paper and other controlled sources to ensure responsible forest management.

For more information visit: www.harpercollins.co.uk/green

Printed and bound in Bosnia and Herzegovina by GPS Group

Author: Carol Hilker
Designer: maru studio
Editorial Director: Caitlin Doyle
Production Controller: Megan Donaghy

DISCLAIMER
The publisher urges the reader to drink, eat, and prepare food responsibly. This book features recipes that include eggs. Ensure eggs are fresh and meet local food-standard requirements. Consuming raw eggs may increase the risk of food-borne illnesses. Individuals who are immunocompromised, pregnant, or elderly should use caution. Be advised: some recipes include nuts or other allergens.

MAC & CHEESE

60 SUPER TASTY RECIPES

CAROL HILKER

Contents

Introduction 6

Recipes

The Opening Act

Deep-fried Mac & Cheese Bites	10
Mac & Cheese Brisket Bites	15
Baked Mac & Cheese Bites	19
French Onion Mac & Cheese Soup	20
Mac & Cheese Muffins	23
Mac & Cheese in a Mug	27

The Main Event

Perfect Baked Mac & Cheese	30
Family Stovetop Mac & Cheese	34
Vegan Mac & Cheese	37
3-ingredient Mac & Cheese	38
4-alarm Mac & Cheese	40
Spinach & Artichoke Dip Mac & Cheese	42
Baked Mac & Cheese Pizza Crust	45
Taco Mac & Cheese	46
Taco Seasoning	48
Southern Mac & Cheese	49
Cheese Lover's 5-cheese Mac	52
Slow Cooker White Cheddar Mac & Cheese	55
Slow Cooker Broccoli-cheddar Mac & Cheese	56
Slow Cooker Pulled Pork Mac & Cheese	59
Texas BBQ Buffet	62
Coleslaw	64
BBQ Baked Beans	65
Cajun Mac & Cheese	66
Lasagne Mac	69
Chicken Parmesan Mac	70
Monticello Mac & Cheese	73
Truffle Mac & Cheese	74
Chili Mac & Cheese	77
Mozzarella Mac & Cheese (Caprese)	78
Jalapeño Pepper Mac & Cheese	80
Mac & Carbonara	82
Pesto Mac & Cheese	85
Homemade Pesto	87
Skillet Cheeseburger Mac	88
Fancy Mac & Cheese	91

Lobster Mac & Cheese 93
Pumpkin Mac & Cheese 97
Bacon & Blue Cheese Mac 98
Philly (Mac &) Cheese Steak 101
Vegas-style Mac & Cheese 102
Chicken Pot Pie Mac & Cheese 105
Wild Mushroom Mac & Cheese 106
Stuffed Mac & Cheese 108
Meat Lover's Mac & Cheese
    (Three Little Pigs Mac) 111
Sriracha & Shrimp Mac & Cheese 115
Buttermilk & Sourdough Mac & Cheese 117
    Easy Sourdough Bread 119
Pizza Mac Bake 120
Buffalo Chicken Mac & Cheese 123
    Buffalo Sauce 125
Skillet Bacon Primavera Mac & Cheese 126
Oktoberfest Mac & Cheese 128

The Second Stage

Breakfast Mac & Cheese 133
Mac & Cheese Waffles 135
Mac My Burger 138
    Mac & Cheese Burger Buns 139
    Mac & Cheese Stuffed Burgers 140
    Mac & Cheese Topping 141
Mexican Street Corn Mac & Cheese 142
Cauliflower Mac & Cheese 144

WASTE NOT:
Ideas for Leftover Mac & Cheese

Tips for Reviving Leftover Mac & Cheese 149
L.O.s Recipes:
    Simple Mac & Cheese Toastie 150
    Pulled Pork MC Sandwich 153
    Breakfast Egg & Mac Muffins 154
    Mac & Cheese Bacon Cups 155

Index 156
Acknowledgments 160
Picture Credits 160

Introduction

A far cry from the boxed, neon 'barely food' staple of yesteryear, today's mac and cheese is now a culinary supernova.

In the past decade, mac and cheese has become indispensable on menus across the globe, from dive diners to artisan eateries, delectable dinner parties to favoured food trucks. So loved is this cheesy goodness, it served as both a simple side and a magnificent masterpiece in its own right. There are even restaurants solely devoted to the dish.

Mac and cheese has come a long way since its origin. The first cheese and pasta pairing came in the form of a casserole. The casseroles were originally served up in Italy during the 14th century, with the first recorded recipe appearing in an Italian cookbook called *Liber de Coquina*. While that 'pasta and cheese dish' is a far cry from what we consider mac and cheese in the 21st century, a dish that boasted the perfect mix of cheese and pasta was born. Another cookbook from 14th-century medieval England, *Forme of Cury*, also had its own version of the dish. That dish was a little more in tune with today's mac and cheese incarnation. Six centuries ago, you may have found 'fresh, hand-cut pasta sandwiched between a mixture of butter and cheese' on the dinner tables of many English royalty.

Since its addition to cuisine, the evolution of mac and cheese took on a life of its own. Like so many beloved dishes, almost every chef (famous or not) has put a spin on pasta and cheese. It's a flexible dish that lacks fussiness. It's a dish that can be well-planned and elevated to include expensive and rare cheeses, or it can be an every person's dish – and for many home cooks, it can help use up the contents of leftover cheese. It can be made on the hob, in the oven, in a vat of oil, or in the microwave, and for some of us, the taste of a boxed mac and cheese can bring back memories of childhood.

This book serves as a road map. The recipes can be followed exactly, or can be mixed and matched with a variety of pasta and different types of cheese. Additionally, this book offers inspiration for what to do with leftovers. Most importantly, this book stands as a love letter to the dish, and one that is so very deserved. Mac and cheese is like an old friend – it makes you feel full and content, it's fun and lively, and you will want to introduce it to many people.

With MAC & CHEESE, learn to make the ultimate comfort food in 60 recipes at home – from Deep-fried Mac & Cheese Bites and Family Stovetop Mac & Cheese, to Breakfast Mac & Cheese and Sriracha & Prawn Mac & Cheese – ideal for a swanky dinner party or a quick weekday meal. Across these mouthwatering pages, discover how to prepare this glorious dish to suit your personal taste, plans, and cooking level – and ability to think outside the box! (Pun intended.)

The recipes in this book are mostly made using cheese sauces with a roux base to which cheese is added, resulting in a smooth finish. However, for supreme meltability, you may want to consider adding a touch of sodium citrate to your cheese sauce. It's the closest food scientists and chefs have been able to get to recreating the smooth cheesiness of boxed mac and cheese. Happy mac-and-cheesing!

Recipes

The Opening Act

DEEP-FRIED MAC & CHEESE BITES

COOK TIME: ABOUT 1 HOUR
(plus chill time)
MAKES: ABOUT 20-30
BITES

1 full mac and cheese
recipe (I like the Perfect
Baked or the Jalapeño
Pepper)
450g cooked bacon,
crumbled or chopped into
small pieces (optional)
3 eggs, beaten
400g crushed croutons or
Panko breadcrumbs
Rapeseed or vegetable oil,
for frying
Salt, for sprinkling

Fried mac and cheese bites are the perfect starter, snack, or Happy Hour bite. You can step this recipe up a notch by adding bacon! The trick to really good mac and cheese bites is to keep the heat consistent and to be patient while cooking. You'll want to wait at least five minutes for these to cool before eating, as hard as it will be to do!

1 Using one full recipe of mac and cheese of your choice, chill the finished mac in the fridge for 6 hours. (Note: if using leftover mac and cheese, chilling for about an hour or two will be sufficient.) If using bacon, combine the bacon and mac and cheese in a large bowl and mix together before setting in the fridge to chill, as above.

2 Set up a bowl with your beaten eggs, another bowl with your breadcrumbs, and get out an ice cream scoop or portion measurer. You'll also want to set out a baking tray covered with baking paper or foil.

3 Remove the mac and cheese from the fridge and, with your hands or a large ice cream scoop, form it into tight balls. You will have about 24 balls, depending on how big you make them. Working one at a time, dip each ball into the eggs, turning to coat evenly and shaking off the excess. Dip the ball into the breadcrumbs and roll to coat in an even layer. Place the breadcrumb-coated mac and cheese ball onto a baking sheet in a single layer. Repeat until all the mac and cheese is used. After freezing for at least 4 hours, you can transfer the balls to an airtight container and keep them in the freezer until ready to fry.

4 When ready to cook, fill a large heavy-bottomed saucepan with oil, leaving 5cm from the surface of the oil to the top of the pan for safety. Heat the oil over a medium–low heat until it hits 160°C on a sugar or meat thermometer.

5 While the oil is heating, preheat the oven to 180°C/Fan 160°C/Gas 4.

6 Working carefully, so as to not burn yourself, add a macaroni and cheese ball to the oil using a long-handled slotted spoon. Fry, rolling the balls as needed, until golden brown all over.

7 Carefully remove the balls from the oil with the slotted spoon and set on a rack over a baking sheet to drain. Then transfer to a second baking sheet in the oven to keep warm while you cook the rest, adding no more than 4 balls at a time into the oil (this will keep the oil temperature even). Allow the last ball to cool for at least 3 minutes before serving. Sprinkle the deep-fried macaroni and cheese with salt and serve hot.

MAC & CHEESE BRISKET BITES

**COOK TIME: 45 MINUTES +
BRISKET COOK TIME (6–8
HOURS)**

MAKES: 20 BITES

FOR THE BRISKET

450–900g beef brisket

½ tbsp olive oil (or a
neutral oil like vegetable
or rapeseed)

FOR THE RUB

½ tbsp soft brown sugar

1 tsp ground paprika

½ tsp onion powder

1 tsp garlic powder

¼ tsp ground cumin

¼ tsp mustard powder

½ tsp salt

¼ tsp freshly ground black
pepper

250ml beef stock

FOR THE BITES

1 full mac and cheese
recipe

3 eggs, whisked

320g crushed croutons
or Panko breadcrumbs

Rapeseed or vegetable oil,
for frying

Parsley, to garnish
(optional)

Barbecue sauce, for
dipping (optional)

Now that you've mastered delicious Mac & Cheese Bites (with or without bacon), the meat lovers among us can delight in adding brisket to take this dish to another level. As with the previous bites recipe, the trick is to keep the heat as consistent as possible and to allow the fried bites to cool a little before eating. This recipe is great for fresh or leftover mac and cheese.

1 Combine the rub ingredients and massage them all over the brisket. Leave to rest for 30 minutes–24 hours in the fridge.

2 Set the slow cooker to low and cook for 6–8 hours. When finished, remove the brisket and place on a baking tray.

3 Preheat the oven to 200°C/Fan 180°C/Gas 6.

4 Pour the liquid from the slow cooker into a saucepan. Bring to a simmer over a medium–high heat and reduce until it thickens to a syrup consistency (it thickens more as it cools).

5 Drizzle the brisket with oil then roast in the oven for 15 minutes until brown spots appear. Remove then baste generously with the sauce and return to the oven for 5 minutes. Remove and baste again, then return to the oven for 5–10 minutes until it caramelizes. Slice the brisket thinly across the grain.

6 If using the brisket for mac and cheese, shred and chop 450g of brisket. In a large bowl, mix the brisket into the mac and cheese. Cover with cling film and chill in the fridge for 6 hours. (If using leftover mac and cheese, chilling for 1–2 hours will be sufficient.)

continues overleaf

7 Set up a bowl with your whisked eggs, another bowl with the breadcrumbs, and an ice cream scoop or portion measurer. You'll want to set out a baking tray covered with baking paper or foil.

8 Remove the mac and cheese from the fridge and, with your hands or a large ice cream scoop, form it into tight balls. You will have about 24 balls depending on how big you make them. Working one at a time, dip each ball into the eggs, turning to coat evenly, then shake off any excess. Dip in the breadcrumbs and roll an even layer to coat. Place onto the baking sheet. Repeat the steps until all the mac and cheese is used.

9 Arrange the baking sheet in the freezer to allow the balls to freeze in a single layer. After freezing for at least 4 hours, you can store the balls in an airtight container in the freezer until ready to fry or fill a large heavy-bottomed saucepan with oil, leaving 5cm from the surface of the oil to the top of the pan for safety.

10 Heat the oil over a medium–low heat until it hits 180°C on a sugar or meat thermometer. While the oil is heating, preheat the oven to 180°C/Fan 160°C/Gas 4.

11 Working carefully, lower a mac and cheese ball using a long-handled slotted spoon. Fry, rolling as needed, until golden brown all over. Carefully remove the mac and cheese ball from the oil with a slotted spoon and set on a rack over a baking sheet to drain. Keep warm on a second baking sheet in the warm oven.

12 Repeat the steps, adding no more than four balls at a time to the oil (this will keep the oil temperature even) until all the bites are fried. Allow the last ball to cool for at least 3 minutes before serving. Sprinkle the bites with salt and optional parsley, and serve hot with barbecue sauce.

BAKED MAC & CHEESE BITES

COOK TIME: 30 MINUTES

MAKES: 20–30 PIECES IF USING A FULL RECIPE OF MAC AND CHEESE

Butter, for greasing

Mac and cheese recipe of your choice (or leftover Perfect Baked, Old Fashioned or Southern Mac & Cheese)

60–115g leftover grated cheese of your choice

Dipping sauce of your choice

Mac and cheese is one of those dishes that doesn't really make fabulous reheated leftovers. While adding a bit of water or milk usually helps, being creative with it is a fantastic way to make the best of any uneaten mac and cheese – feel free to use any leftover recipe you desire to make these bites. These can be made in the oven (use the convection if you have that setting) or in an air fryer – follow the manufacturer's instructions on bake time. These are great to bring to a party or bring-a-dish event.

1 Preheat the oven to 200°C/Fan 180°C/Gas 6. Butter a couple of mini muffin tins.

2 Using a small portion scoop or small ice cream scoop, spoon portions of the mac and cheese into the mini muffin tin cups, stuffing to the top edge, then top each with a small sprinkle of grated cheese.

3 Bake for 20 minutes, or until the tops of the mac and cheese bites are turning golden brown and crisp up. (The key to these bites is to make them small so they can crisp up on the outside.)

4 Allow the mac and cheese bites to set and cool a little in the tin for about 5 minutes, then pop them out by running a knife around the edges or use your fingers. Serve immediately with your choice of dipping sauce on the side, such as BBQ, marinara or tomato sauce.

FRENCH ONION MAC & CHEESE SOUP

COOK TIME: ABOUT 1 HOUR
SERVES: 4

4 tbsp unsalted butter

4 medium brown onions, thinly sliced

Coarse sea salt and freshly ground black pepper, to taste

1 bay leaf

2–3 sprigs thyme

250ml dry white wine

1 tbsp cognac (optional)

1 litre veal or beef stock

1 x Family Stovetop Mac & Cheese, subbing Gruyère for the Cheddar

25g grated Gruyère cheese

25g grated Parmesan cheese

1 baguette, cut into 2.5–5-cm wide slices, lightly spread with melted butter (or use garlic butter croutons)

This 'soup' is a beautiful pairing to mac and cheese. It's also a way to take a simple dish and add a little flair. The caramelized onions, stock, and deep flavours of the wine and cognac pair masterfully with the Gruyère cheese. This is a great dish for a cold winter night or crisp autumn weekend afternoon.

1 Melt the butter in a large saucepan over a medium heat. Add half of the onions and season with ¼ teaspoon salt and a few grinds of pepper. Top with the remaining onions and season with ¼ teaspoon salt and a few more grinds of pepper. Add the bay leaf and thyme sprigs. Cook, stirring occasionally, until all of the liquid evaporates and the onions are very soft and just beginning to turn golden, about 45 minutes–1 hour.

2 Add the white wine and cognac, if using, bring to a simmer and cook, stirring, until almost completely evaporated, about 6 minutes. Pour in the stock and 250ml water, bring to a high simmer, and cook until the soup has reduced to about 1.2 litres, about 30–40 minutes.

3 Season with salt and a few grinds of pepper and remove the bay leaves and thyme. Either keep warm over a low heat or leave to cool completely, refrigerate, and reheat later. (The soup can be made and refrigerated up to two days in advance or frozen for up to a month.)

Use any mac recipe or leftover mac. I recommend the Family Stovetop Mac or the Slow Cooker White Cheddar Mac. Sub Gruyère for the Cheddar in whatever recipe you use!

4 To build the dish, preheat the grill. Place the soup crocks on a rimmed baking sheet and divide the hot soup among them, filling each about three-quarters full. Top each with a quarter of the mac and cheese (some will sink into the soup, which is fine). Evenly sprinkle with the cheeses and the baguette slices or croutons on top. Grill for 2–3 minutes until the cheese is melted and golden brown in spots (the soup will bubble and some may spill out). Serve hot.

MAC & CHEESE MUFFINS

COOK TIME: 1 HOUR

MAKES 12 MUFFINS

450g elbow macaroni or other small pasta

½ tsp olive oil or melted butter

115g unsalted butter, plus extra for greasing

1.2 litres whole milk

60g plain flour

2 tsp salt

¼ tsp freshly ground black pepper

¼ tsp freshly grated nutmeg

¼ tsp garlic powder

Splash of hot sauce, or to taste (optional)

500g grated mature and/or white Cheddar cheese

230g grated mild Cheddar cheese or 125g grated Pecorino Romano cheese

1 bag (350g) garlic butter croutons

This recipe is sure to be a hit for grown-ups and kids alike. Mac and cheese is so much more fun when it is cooked in a muffin or cupcake tin, so it's the perfect kid-size or on-the-go portion. For the ideal muffin, let the mac cool in the pan for about ten minutes before removing, then it won't fall apart. The muffins can be eaten immediately, or leave them to cool and then wrap individually for a quick snack.

1 Cook the macaroni in a pan of boiling water for 2–3 minutes less than the instructions on the packet, until al dente. Tip the macaroni into a colander, rinse under cold running water, and drain well. Drizzle ½ teaspoon of olive oil or melted butter on top, then toss and mix thoroughly. This will stop the pasta sticking together.

2 Preheat the oven to 190°C/Fan 170°C/Gas 5. Lightly butter a large 12-hole muffin tin or small 24-hole muffin or cupcake tin.

3 Heat the milk in a medium saucepan over a low–medium heat.

4 In a separate high-sided frying pan or large saucepan, melt the butter over a low–medium heat. When the butter bubbles, add the flour. Cook, whisking the butter and flour for 1 minute. Once the mixture (roux) has thickened, slowly pour in the hot milk, about 60ml at a time, whisking constantly, until the mixture bubbles and becomes a thick sauce. You may have to turn the heat down if the sauce thickens too quickly, use your best judgment.

continues overleaf

5 Once the sauce has thickened, remove the pan from the heat. Stir in the salt, black pepper, nutmeg, garlic powder, hot sauce, if using, and all but 115–155g Cheddar cheese (or 50g Parmesan, if using). Mix until a smooth sauce forms, then stir in the macaroni.

6 Spoon the mixture into the greased muffin tins – or you can use muffin cups. Pulse the croutons in a food processor to breadcrumbs. Sprinkle the remaining Cheddar and the breadcrumbs over the top. Bake until the cheese has browned, about 30 minutes. Cool for at least 5 minutes, then serve hot.

This recipe is sure to be a hit for grown-ups and kids alike.

MAC & CHEESE **IN A MUG**

COOK TIME: 5 MINUTES
SERVES 1

28g elbow macaroni

4 tbsp whole milk

½ tsp cornflour

30g grated mild or mature
  Cheddar cheese

Salt and freshly ground
  black pepper, to taste

Perfect for a quick lunch and easy enough for kids to make, this recipe uses six ingredients and can be put together in less than five minutes. The secret is to use a thickener. I usually prefer to use freshly grated cheese and the cornflour mix (as stated below); however, if you have pre-grated cheese in your fridge that you'd like to get rid of, feel free to use it in place of freshly grated – just omit the cornflour.

1 In a large microwavable mug (225g or larger) or small bowl, combine the macaroni and 175ml cold water. You need a large mug as the water will boil and rise up. Microwave for about 3½ minutes – you want the pasta to be fully cooked. Drain off the remaining cooking water.

2 Stir the milk, cornflour, and grated cheese into the pasta in the mug and microwave for a final 60 seconds to create the sauce. Leave to stand for 10 seconds and stir well. Season to taste with salt and pepper.

Quick and easy five-minute recipe kids can make.

Recipes

The Main Event

PERFECT BAKED MAC & CHEESE

COOK TIME: ABOUT 1 HOUR

SERVES: 4–6 (PLUS LEFTOVERS)

450g elbow macaroni

½ tsp olive oil or melted butter

1.2 litres semi-skimmed or whole milk

115g unsalted butter, plus extra for greasing

60g plain flour

2 tsp salt

¼ tsp freshly ground black pepper

¼ tsp freshly grated nutmeg

¼ tsp garlic powder

Pinch of chipotle chilli powder, or to taste (optional)

500g grated mature and/or white Cheddar cheese

230g grated mild Cheddar cheese or 125g grated Pecorino Romano cheese

1 bag (350g) garlic butter croutons (optional)

If you make just one recipe from this book, let it be this. It's really flexible because the cheeses can be swapped out for whatever you have on hand. While I don't usually use Gruyère, I can attest that it can be an absolute star if you swap it in for 115g of the grated mature Cheddar when making the cheese sauce. One pro tip: when combining the pasta with the sauce, you might feel like there is too much sauce; however, when you remove the final product from the oven, you will see it will have thickened and the pasta will have baked a touch more.

1 Cook the macaroni in a pan of boiling water for 2–3 minutes less than the instructions on the packet, until al dente. Tip the macaroni into a colander, rinse under cold running water, and drain well. Drizzle ½ teaspoon of olive oil or melted butter on top, then toss and mix thoroughly. This will stop the pasta sticking together.

2 Heat the milk in a medium saucepan over a low–medium heat.

3 In a separate high-sided frying pan or large saucepan, melt the butter over a low–medium heat. When the butter bubbles, add the flour and cook, whisking the butter and flour, for about 1 minute. Once the mixture (roux) has thickened, slowly pour in the hot milk a little at a time, whisking constantly, until the mixture bubbles and becomes a thick sauce. You may have to turn the heat down if the sauce thickens too quickly, use your best judgment!

4 Preheat the oven to 190°C/Fan 170°C/Gas 5. Lightly butter a 3-litre casserole dish.

5 Once the sauce has thickened, remove the pan from the heat. Stir in the salt, black pepper, nutmeg, garlic powder, chipotle chilli powder, if using, and all but 115–155g Cheddar cheese (or 50g Parmesan, if using). Mix until a smooth sauce forms, then stir in the cooked macaroni.

6 Pour the mixture into the baking dish. If using, pulse the croutons in a food processor to breadcrumbs. Sprinkle the remaining Cheddar cheese (or Parmesan) and breadcrumbs, if using, over the top. Bake until the cheese has browned, about 30 minutes. Cool for at least 5 minutes before serving.

If you make just one recipe from this book, let it be this.

FAMILY STOVETOP MAC & CHEESE

COOK TIME: 30 MINUTES

SERVES: 4–6 (PLUS LEFTOVERS)

450g elbow macaroni

½ tsp olive oil or melted butter

1.2 litres semi-skimmed or whole milk

115g unsalted butter

60g plain flour

2 tsp salt

¼ tsp freshly ground black pepper

¼ tsp freshly grated nutmeg

¼ tsp garlic powder

Pinch of cayenne or chipotle chilli powder, or to taste (optional)

500g grated mature and/or white Cheddar cheese

230g grated mild Cheddar cheese or 125g grated Pecorino Romano cheese

If this recipe looks familiar, it's because it's similar to the recipe for the Perfect Baked Mac & Cheese, except you leave out the croutons and baking and cook the pasta all the way through first. Learn this base recipe, and you can perfect many others in this book – from Breakfast Mac & Cheese to Sriracha & Prawn Mac & Cheese. Similar to the baked version, this recipe is extremely flexible in using whatever cheeses YOU like and have on hand.

1 Cook the macaroni in a pan of boiling water, following the instructions on the packet, until al dente. Tip the macaroni into a colander, rinse under cold running water, and drain well. Drizzle ½ teaspoon of olive oil or melted butter on top, then toss and mix thoroughly. This will stop the pasta sticking together.

2 Heat the milk in a medium saucepan over a low–medium heat.

3 In a separate high-sided frying pan or large saucepan, melt the butter over a low–medium heat. When the butter bubbles, add the flour and cook, whisking the butter and flour for about 1 minute. Once the mixture (roux) has thickened, slowly pour in the hot milk a little at a time, whisking constantly, until the mixture bubbles and becomes a thick sauce. You may have to turn the heat down if the sauce thickens too quickly, use your best judgment.

4 Once the sauce has thickened, remove the pan from heat. Stir in the salt, black pepper, nutmeg, garlic powder, cayenne or chipotle, if using, and all but 115–155g Cheddar cheese (or 50g Parmesan, if using). Mix until a smooth cheese sauce forms. Once smooth, stir in the cooked macaroni and coat with the sauce, then cook on low for a few minutes to thicken. Serve hot!

VEGAN MAC & CHEESE

COOK TIME: 20 MINUTES

SERVES: 4–6

240g raw unsalted cashews

450g pasta shells or elbow macaroni

2 tsp salt

2 tsp garlic powder

2 tsp onion powder

½ tsp chilli powder

½ tsp smoked paprika

60g nutritional yeast

750ml unsweetened almond milk

2 tsp Dijon mustard

1 tbsp vegan butter

50g Panko or Italian breadcrumbs

1 tsp dried thyme

How do you make an amazing mac and cheese without cheese? Cashews and nutritional yeast. These ingredients create the kind of cheese sauce that makes you re-think all of your food choices. Even the biggest mac and cheese enthusiast will be able to see the merit in this recipe.

1 Preheat the oven to 190°C/Fan 170°C/Gas 5 and bring a large saucepan of water to a rolling boil for the pasta.

2 Place the cashews in a small or medium bowl. Using a ladle, remove 250ml boiling water from the pan and pour it over your cashews. Leave to soak for 15 minutes until they are soft.

3 Add the pasta to the boiling water and cook for 3 minutes less than the instructions on the packet, until al dente. Drain and set aside.

4 In a small bowl, stir together the salt, garlic, onion, and chilli powders, and paprika.

5 Drain the cashews and transfer to a blender or food processor. Add the spice mixture, nutritional yeast, 500ml of the almond milk, and mustard. Blend on high speed until creamy. Add the remaining 250ml almond milk and blend again. The sauce should be very thin.

6 Toss the cooked pasta into the vegan cheese sauce, then pour mixture into a 3-litre baking dish.

7 To make the breadcrumb topping, heat the vegan butter in a small saucepan over a medium heat, then add the breadcrumbs and thyme and cook until lightly golden. Sprinkle over the macaroni.

8 Bake the mac and cheese for 10 minutes, then cool slightly before serving hot.

3-INGREDIENT MAC & CHEESE

COOK TIME: 30 MINUTES
SERVES: 4-6

350g macaroni shells or
pasta of your choice

½ tsp olive oil or melted
butter

1 x 350ml can evaporated
milk

350g grated mild or
medium Cheddar cheese

Salt and freshly ground
black pepper, to taste

Parsley, to garnish
(optional)

For those who indulge in the guilty pleasure of making Kraft or other boxed mac and cheese, this recipe is for you! This mac and cheese is not only easy, it's almost too good to be as simple as it actually is. The combination of evaporated milk and Cheddar makes an incredible base for a quick cheese sauce that can be stirred into pasta, used to dip chips into, or to pour over a plate of nachos. This recipe is close to my heart because it reminds me of the gooey, squeezy cheese you squeeze out of a packet and mix into hot noodles.

1 Cook the macaroni in a pan of boiling water following the instructions on the packet, until al dente. Tip the macaroni into a colander, rinse under cold running water, and drain well. Drizzle ½ teaspoon of olive oil or melted butter on top, then toss and mix thoroughly. This will stop the pasta sticking together.

2 Bring the evaporated milk to the boil in a medium saucepan over a medium–high heat. Add the cheese and immediately reduce the heat to low, whisking constantly until the cheese has melted and the liquid has thickened to a creamy sauce, about 2 minutes. Add salt and pepper to taste, if needed, or optional parsley garnish.

For those whose guilty pleasure is boxed mac and cheese, this recipe of pasta, evaporated milk, and cheese is for you!

4-ALARM MAC & CHEESE

COOK TIME: ABOUT 1 HOUR
SERVES: 4-6

450g macaroni shells
½ tsp olive oil or melted butter
115g unsalted butter, plus extra for greasing
1.2 litres whole milk
60g plain flour
1 jalapeño chilli, deseeded and diced

Spice is one of those things that you either love or hate. If you're a fan of heat, this 4-alarm Mac & Cheese was made for you – while simple in preparation, the flavour is bold. This recipe uses Cheddar with chilli and Gouda cheeses, chipotle chilli powder, and cayenne. Try substituting croutons or breadcrumbs for spicy corn chips for the crunch on top – it might sound unusual, but I highly recommend it.

1 Cook the macaroni in a pan of boiling water for 2–3 minutes less than the instructions on the packet, until al dente. Tip the macaroni into a colander, rinse under cold running water, and drain

2 tsp salt

¼ tsp freshly ground black pepper

¼ tsp chipotle chilli powder

¼ tsp cayenne pepper

30g grated mature Cheddar with chilli

230g grated Gouda or mild Cheddar

1 bag (350g) garlic butter croutons (optional)

well. Drizzle ½ teaspoon of olive oil or melted butter on top, then toss and mix thoroughly. This will stop the pasta sticking together.

2 Preheat the oven to 190°C/Fan 170°C/Gas 5. Lightly butter a 3-litre casserole dish and set the dish aside.

3 Heat the milk in a medium saucepan over a low–medium heat.

4 In a separate high-sided frying pan or large saucepan, melt the butter over a low–medium heat. When the butter bubbles, add the flour. Cook, whisking the butter and flour for about 1 minute. Once the mixture (roux) has thickened, slowly pour in the hot milk about 60ml at a time, whisking constantly, until the mixture bubbles and becomes a thick sauce. You may have to turn the heat down if the sauce thickens too quickly, use your best judgment. Add the diced jalapeño chilli.

5 Once the sauce has thickened, remove the pan from the heat. Stir in the salt, black pepper, chipotle, cayenne, and all but 115g of the Cheddar with chilli and the Gouda or Cheddar. Mix until a smooth cheese sauce forms, then stir in the drained macaroni.

6 Transfer the mixture to the baking dish. If using, pulse the croutons in a food processor to breadcrumbs. Sprinkle the remaining cheese and the breadcrumbs over the top. Bake until the cheese has browned, about 30 minutes. Cool for at least 5 minutes, then serve hot.

SPINACH & ARTICHOKE DIP
MAC & CHEESE

COOK TIME: 1 HOUR
SERVES: 4-6

450g pasta of your choice
½ tsp olive oil, plus 1 tbsp
    for frying
115g unsalted butter, plus
    extra for greasing
2 cloves garlic, finely
    chopped
65g diced brown onion
2 x 400-g cans artichoke
    quarters, drained
1.2 litres whole milk
60g plain flour
2 tsp salt
¼ tsp freshly ground black
    pepper
¼ tsp garlic powder
500g grated fontina or
    mozzarella cheese
125g grated Pecorino
    Romano cheese
55g soft goat's cheese
350g fresh or frozen
    spinach

Spinach & Artichoke Dip Mac & Cheese is like two friends you have been wanting to fix up for years. Each is the ideal complement to the other, and once introduced, they are destined for happiness together. And isn't that what we should all be seeking in a partner – someone to complement you and enhance you?

1 Cook the macaroni in a pan of boiling water for 2–3 minutes less than the instructions on the packet, until al dente. Tip the macaroni into a colander, rinse under cold running water, and drain well. Drizzle ½ teaspoon of olive oil or melted butter on top, then toss and mix thoroughly. This will stop the pasta sticking together.

2 Preheat the oven to 190°C/Fan 170°C/Gas 5. Lightly butter a 3-litre casserole dish.

3 In a casserole dish or large, deep saucepan, heat the 1 tablespoon olive oil over a medium-high heat. Add the garlic, onion, and artichokes and sauté just until lightly browned, about 4 minutes. Remove from the pan and set aside.

4 Heat the milk in a medium saucepan over a low–medium heat.

5 In the same pan the artichokes were cooked in, melt the butter over a low–medium heat. When the butter bubbles, add the flour. Cook, whisking the butter and flour for about 1 minute.

6 Once the mixture (roux) has thickened, slowly pour in the hot milk about 60ml at a time, whisking constantly, until the mixture bubbles and becomes a thick sauce. You may have to turn the

heat down if the sauce thickens too quickly, use your best judgment.

7 Once the sauce has thickened, remove the pan from the heat. Stir in the salt, black pepper, garlic powder, and all but 115–155g of your fontina and Parmesan cheeses. Mix until a smooth sauce forms, then add the goat's cheese and stir until smooth and combined. Stir in the macaroni, then add the onion, garlic, and artichoke mixture, then the spinach (fresh or frozen is fine – fresh will wilt down in the oven and frozen will give some more flavour).

8 Tip the mixture into the casserole dish. Sprinkle the remaining cheese over the top and bake until the cheese has browned, about 30 minutes. Cool for at least 5 minutes, then serve hot.

BAKED MAC & CHEESE PIZZA CRUST

COOK TIME: 45 MINUTES

SERVES: 4–6

1 x 3-ingredient Mac & Cheese (page 38)

2 large eggs, beaten

Non-stick cooking spray, olive oil, or butter, for greasing

225g minced Italian sausage (optional)

95g chopped onion

250–310ml pizza sauce

28 pepperoni slices (optional)

110g grated mozzarella cheese

110g grated Parmesan or Asiago cheese

Italian seasoning and chilli flakes, to taste (optional)

A fun project for kids or an interesting meal or side dish, this baked mac and cheese pizza will be the talk of the dinner. For a homemade pizza night, swap out your favourite crust recipe for this mac and cheese pizza crust. Add Italian sausage, pepperoni, and any toppings of your choice for the perfect mix of pizza and mac and cheese.

1 Preheat the oven to 190°C/Fan 170°C/Gas 5.

2 Make the 3-ingredient Mac & Cheese (page 38). After the mac and cheese is done, stir in the 2 eggs and incorporate well, then set aside.

3 Grease a 30-cm pizza pan or baking sheet with cooking spray, olive oil, or butter. Spread the mac and cheese mixture onto the greased pan, then bake for 10 minutes. Remove from the oven, and while the crust partially cooks, in a large frying pan, cook the sausage, if using, and onion over a medium heat until the meat is no longer pink. Crumble the meat and drain off any fat. Stir in the pizza sauce.

4 Spread the meat and sauce mixture over the macaroni crust. Sprinkle over the pepperoni or other toppings, then bake for 10–15 minutes until the cheese is melted and golden. Allow to cool for 5 minutes. If you like, sprinkle with Italian seasoning or chilli flakes.

TACO MAC & CHEESE

COOK TIME: 45 MINUTES
SERVES: 4–6

450g minced beef
25g taco seasoning
(packet or homemade,
page 48)
1 x 3-ingredient Mac
& Cheese (page 38)

TO SERVE (OPTIONAL)
6–8 hard or soft taco shells
(flour or corn will both
work)
55g shredded lettuce
2 tomatoes, diced
120ml sour cream
115g grated Cheddar
cheese
Guacamole and salsa,
if desired
Coriander or parsley,
to garnish (optional)

This mac and cheese is a great choice for those home cooks who have an indecisive streak. Maybe you want tacos but also want mac and cheese – if you've ever had that dilemma, well, this is your signature dish. Combining cheese, minced beef, taco seasoning, and all your favourite taco fixings into a mac and cheese means no need for a tortilla. But if you want the full taco experience, add this as a filling to a tortilla to make a Mac & Cheese Burrito, or to a hard-shell taco for a Taco Supreme. Salsa and guacamole especially will take this mac to the next level.

1 Make the 3-ingredient Mac & Cheese, preferably using a three-cheese taco blend including mature Cheddar, Cheddar with chilli, and Gouda, but you can use any cheese you like. You can make the pasta and then move on with the recipe, or just go ahead and proceed through the entire mac and cheese recipe and use as much as you need. There are recipes for your leftover mac and cheese on pages 150–55. In a large frying pan over a medium–high heat, brown the minced beef, breaking it up with a wooden spoon or spatula as it cooks. Once the meat has cooked and browned, sprinkle over your taco seasoning (or make homemade, page 48), and 150ml water. Cook, uncovered, until the water has cooked off and the taco seasoning is well incorporated. Mix well and remove from the heat. It should be well cooked and have no liquid left over.

2 Combine the minced beef with the 3-ingredient Mac & Cheese. If eating as a dish in its own right, add to a plate or bowl and garnish. Alternatively, fill a soft tortilla or hard-shell taco and add some lettuce, tomatoes, sour cream, grated cheese, guacamole, salsa, and herbs to garnish, if using.

Taco Seasoning

COOK TIME: 5 MINUTES

MAKES: 2½ TABLESPOONS

1 tbsp chilli powder
1 tsp ground cumin
1½ tsp sea salt
1 tsp freshly ground black pepper
½ tsp paprika
1 tsp garlic powder
½ tsp onion powder
½ tsp crushed chilli flakes
¼ tsp dried oregano

This taco seasoning is extremely versatile. It can be used for tacos or as a seasoning added directly to a cheese sauce. This taco seasoning can also be used for burgers, enchiladas, or burritos. Add it to a mixture of leftover cheese, melt on low on the hob, and make yourself an amazing plate of nachos.

1 Combine all the ingredients in a small bowl and whisk with a fork. Store in a small sealable sandwich bag or spice jar for a maximum of six months.

SOUTHERN MAC & CHEESE

COOK TIME: 1 HOUR
SERVES: 4-6

450g elbow macaroni or cavatappi

250ml whole milk

2 x 350ml cans evaporated milk

3 eggs, lightly beaten

1 tsp salt, or to taste

1 tbsp freshly ground black pepper

115g unsalted butter, cut into small pieces

6 tbsp sour cream

450g mild Cheddar or Red Leicester, cut into small chunks (or sliced Cheddar will also work)

350g grated Gouda and/or Cheddar with chilli cheese, plus 115g for topping

175g grated mature Cheddar cheese

This mac and cheese recipe may seem untraditional to some. It's not your average saucy mac, more of a macaroni pasta and cheese casserole. While many of us like our mac and cheese creamy, this one is baked, with the cheeses melting together to thicken the base and cushion the pasta, following the method that is often used in the American South. While you might be hesitant to experiment, give this a go, as this delicious dish is a perfect side for Sunday dinners, bring-a-dish parties, and holidays (I'm looking at you, Christmas!). It also makes the perfect base for baking or frying into Baked Mac & Cheese Bites (page 19).

1 Preheat the oven to 220°C/Fan 200°C/Gas 7.

2 Cook the macaroni in a pan of boiling water for 2–3 minutes less than the instructions on the packet, until al dente. Tip the macaroni into a colander, rinse under cold running water, and drain well. Transfer the drained pasta to a large baking dish.

3 In the same saucepan, whisk together the whole milk, evaporated milk, eggs, salt, and pepper until combined. Pour the mixture over the cooked macaroni in the dish. Add the butter, sour cream, Gouda and mature Cheddar cheeses, reserving 50g to sprinkle on top. Stir to combine well and top evenly with the grated mild Cheddar.

4 Bake for 35–40 minutes until bubbly and lightly browned on top. Leave to rest for 10 minutes or so before serving. Stir if it's really bugging you!

CHEESE LOVER'S 5-CHEESE MAC

COOK TIME: 1 HOUR
SERVES: 4-6

1 large egg
2 x 350ml cans evaporated milk or half the amount of whole milk (350ml)
1 tbsp seasoned salt (or regular salt)
1 tsp freshly grated black pepper
1 tsp garlic powder
1 tsp onion powder
½ tsp mustard powder
½ tsp paprika
¼ tsp chipotle chilli powder (optional)
450g large elbow macaroni
½ tsp olive oil or melted butter, plus extra for greasing
115g unsalted butter, sliced into 1 tbsp pieces
440g grated mild Cheddar, Red Leicester, or American cheese

This recipe is for all of the cheese lovers out there; it packs in more kinds of cheese in a single recipe than any other in the book – in fact, it's an entire cheeseboard in one dish! This is a little more sophisticated and less fussy than the Perfect Baked Mac & Cheese recipe, and allows the cheese to totally melt. What comes out is a delicate creamy-gooey balance of a mac and cheese casserole that highlights all five cheeses used.

1 Preheat the oven to 180°C/Fan 160°C/Gas 4.

2 In a mixing bowl, lightly beat the egg with a whisk. Add the milk, salt, black pepper, garlic, onion and mustard powders, paprika, and chipotle, if using, to the bowl with the egg. Whisk the mixture thoroughly to combine the spices and milk. Set aside.

3 Cook the macaroni in a pan of boiling water for 2–3 minutes less than the instructions on the packet, until al dente. Tip the macaroni into a colander, rinse under cold running water, and drain well. Drizzle ½ teaspoon of olive oil or melted butter on top, then toss and mix thoroughly. This will stop the pasta sticking together. Lightly butter a 3-litre casserole dish.

4 In the same pan you used to cook the macaroni, melt the butter over a medium heat.

5 Once the butter has completely melted, use a spoon to stir the drained macaroni into it.

6 Add the evaporated milk mixture to the macaroni and stir to incorporate. Add half each of the grated mild Cheddar or American cheese, extra-mature Cheddar, smoked Gouda, smoked Gruyère, and plain Gouda to the pan. Stir well to combine – the cheese won't fully melt, but it will become gooey.

290g grated extra-mature Cheddar cheese

290g grated smoked Gouda (or plain)

290g grated smoked Gruyère (or plain) cheese

230g grated plain Gouda

7 Pour half the mixed macaroni into the casserole dish. Sprinkle half the reserved cheese mixture over the macaroni. Cover with a second layer and top with the remaining cheeses. Cover with foil and bake for 30 minutes, then remove the foil and cook for another 25–30 minutes until the cheese starts to bubble and brown slightly. Allow to cool for 10 minutes before serving.

SLOW COOKER WHITE CHEDDAR MAC & CHEESE

COOK TIME: 3½–4 HOURS
SERVES: 4–6

- 450g elbow macaroni or cavatappi
- 76g unsalted butter
- 56g cream cheese
- 1.2 litres whole milk
- 450g grated mature white Cheddar cheese
- 115g grated Cheddar with chilli cheese
- 115g grated Parmesan, mozzarella or an Italian blend cheese

This recipe is easy. It's perfect for a lazy weekend or, if doubled, a bring-a-dish party or gathering (especially when you do not have a lot of time to spend in the kitchen). Just add all the ingredients to your slow cooker, mix, and let the slow cooker do all the work.

1 Pour the macaroni into a slow cooker. Cut the butter and the cream cheese into 5-cm chunks and place on top of the pasta. Add the milk. Stir in all of the cheeses.

2 Cook in a slow cooker on low for 3–4 hours, giving it a stir once an hour. After 3 hours, check every 20 minutes or so until the desired thickness of sauce is reached.

SLOW COOKER BROCCOLI-CHEDDAR MAC & CHEESE

COOK TIME: 3-4 HOURS
SERVES: 4-6

450g elbow macaroni or cavatappi

70g butter

55g cream cheese

1.25 litres whole milk

460g grated mature white Cheddar cheese

115g grated Cheddar with chilli cheese

100g grated Parmesan, mozzarella, or an Italian blend cheese

450g broccoli, cut into 2.5-5-cm pieces

Salt and freshly ground black pepper, to taste (optional)

Now that you have mastered this super-simple slow cooker recipe (page 55), just add some vegetables for a very easy alternative. This recipe is great for mac-and-cheese lovers who may need a little encouragement to eat their greens. (Looking at you, fussy eaters!)

1 Add the macaroni/pasta to a slow cooker. Cut the butter and cream cheese into 5-cm chunks and place on top of the pasta. Add the milk and stir in all of the cheeses. Cook in a slow cooker on low for 3-4 hours. Give it a stir once an hour.

2 After 3 hours, add the broccoli and cook together for 10-20 minutes or so until the desired thickness of sauce is reached. Ten minutes will give al dente broccoli. Serve topped with optional salt and pepper or a garnish.

MAKE IT YOUR OWN
Why not substitute in other favourite vegetables, such as cauliflower, squash, leeks, or peas?

SLOW COOKER PULLED PORK
MAC & CHEESE

COOK TIME: 2 HOURS AND 25 MINUTES
SERVES: 4–6

FOR THE PULLED PORK:

900g boneless pork shoulder, fat trimmed

½ brown onion, sliced

½ can Coke, Dr. Pepper, or Ginger Ale

250–500ml BBQ sauce

FOR THE MAC & CHEESE

Non-stick cooking spray

450g cavatappi

½ tsp olive oil or melted butter

115g unsalted butter

1.2 litres whole milk

115g plain flour

500g grated mature and/or white Cheddar cheese

250g grated mild Cheddar cheese

Slow-cooked pork is one of the best dishes to prepare for a large crowd. This mac and cheese combines savoury and sweet pulled pork with the Perfect Baked Mac & Cheese to create a dish that's ideal for a party or as a main dish for a Sunday dinner. Add baked beans (page 65), sweet potato fries, tater tots, or hash browns, and homemade brownies for a perfect meal.

1 Place the pork shoulder and onion in a 6-litre slow cooker. Pour in the fizzy drink and cook on low for 4–5 hours while you make the mac and cheese.

2 Preheat the oven to 190°C/Fan 170°C/ Gas 5 and spray a 3-litre casserole dish with non-stick spray.

3 Cook the pasta in a pan of boiling water following the instructions on the packet, until al dente. Tip the macaroni into a colander, rinse under cold running water, and drain well. Drizzle ½ teaspoon of olive oil or melted butter on top, then toss and mix thoroughly. This will stop the pasta sticking together.

4 In a large frying pan over a medium heat, heat the butter, and once melted, whisk in the flour and allow to cook for 30 seconds–1 minute. Slowly add the milk a few tablespoons at a time and whisk constantly. After all the milk is added, reduce the heat to low and whisk until the sauce becomes thick and creamy.

continues overleaf

5 Transfer the pork roast from the slow cooker to a large plate and shred with two forks. If there are any large chunks of fat, just remove them. Drain the liquid from the slow cooker and put the shredded pork back into the slow cooker. Add the BBQ sauce and stir to coat. Cover to keep warm while you assemble the mac and cheese.

6 Remove the sauce from the heat and add the cheeses, reserving about 55g to bake on top, stirring until melted and smooth. Stir in the macaroni.

7 Transfer the mac and cheese to the prepared dish and top with the pulled pork. (Top with all, top with half, or top with a little. It's likely there will be leftover pulled pork!) Sprinkle over the remaining cheeses. Bake for about 15 minutes just to help warm the mixture through. Serve with extra BBQ sauce, if you like.

You can add more BBQ sauce if you like. You want the meat to be coated but not dripping with sauce.

Texas BBQ Buffet

Pulled pork and mac and cheese are a pair made in heaven. Try them alongside coleslaw, BBQ baked beans, collard greens, pickles, or any other delicious BBQ pairings to create a Texas BBQ Buffet. It's ideal not only for BBQs and outdoor parties, but game nights and summer parties.

Coleslaw

COOK TIME: 30 MINUTES
SERVES: 4–6

60ml apple cider vinegar
1 tbsp grainy mustard (or Dijon)
1 tbsp honey (or 1 tsp sugar)
60ml good-quality olive oil
½ head of green cabbage, thinly sliced
½ head of red cabbage, thinly sliced
2 large carrots, grated
3 salad or spring onions, thinly sliced
½ tsp salt
¼ tsp freshly ground black pepper

This coleslaw is for anyone out there who doesn't like mayonnaise. The mixture of cabbage, carrot, and onion with a mixture of mustard, honey, salt and pepper makes a crisp topping for a Pulled Pork Mac & Cheese or as a side for any barbecue dish.

1 In a small bowl, whisk together the vinegar, mustard, honey, and olive oil and set aside.

2 In a separate bowl, mix together the cabbages, carrots, and salad or spring onions.

3 Pour a small amount of the dressing onto the cabbage mixture and mix until combined and the desired amount of dressing is achieved. Season with salt and pepper to taste, and chill before serving.

BBQ Baked Beans

COOK TIME: 35 MINUTES
MAKES: 1.1 KILOGRAMS

Rapeseed oil, for frying
225g sliced bacon or brisket (optional)
1 small brown onion, diced
1 yellow or red pepper, deseeded and diced
3 garlic cloves, finely chopped
1 tbsp smoked paprika
½ tsp chilli powder or ¼ teaspoon hot sauce
½ tsp salt
¼ tsp freshly cracked black pepper
3 tbsp apple cider vinegar
2 tbsp BBQ sauce
2 tbsp ketchup
1 tbsp grainy mustard (or Dijon)
1 tbsp soft brown sugar
2 x 600-g cans baked beans

These BBQ Baked Beans will complete almost any bring-a-dish party or barbecue. This recipe can be easily doubled or tripled or be made with almost any leftover meat you have (although pulled pork or brisket are both highly recommended).

1 Preheat the oven to 200°C/Fan 180°C/Gas 6.

2 In a large, ovenproof frying pan, add a bit of oil and warm the bacon or brisket, if using, until crispy.

3 Stir in the onion, pepper, and garlic. Cook, stirring often, until everything softens, about 5 minutes. Stir in the paprika, chilli powder, salt and pepper. Cook for 1–2 minutes. Stir in the vinegar, BBQ sauce, ketchup, mustard, and brown sugar until combined.

4 Add the baked beans directly from the can. Bring the mixture to the boil, then turn off the heat. Place the frying pan (or transfer to an ovenproof dish) in the oven and bake for 30–35 minutes until bubbly and syrup. Allow to cool slightly before serving.

CAJUN MAC & CHEESE

COOK TIME: 1 HOUR
SERVES: 4–6

1 x 450-g packet wagon wheel pasta, or shells, macaroni, or cavatappi

½ tsp olive oil or melted butter

115g unsalted butter, plus extra for greasing

½ tbsp rapeseed oil

½ x 450-g packet andouille sausage, chopped

65g chopped brown or white onion

75g chopped green pepper

75g chopped red pepper

1 tsp finely chopped garlic

1.2 litres whole milk

60g plain flour

2 tsp salt

1 tbsp Cajun seasoning

500g grated medium Cheddar cheese

250g grated Cheddar with chilli cheese

This Cajun Mac & Cheese is just like a visit to the Big Easy – spicy, fun, and full of flavour. It uses andouille sausage (turkey sausage, chicken sausage, or even Italian sausage can be substituted in a pinch), a colourful array of peppers, garlic, and a mix of Cheddar and Cheddar with chilli. A few chicken breasts or some scampi or grilled prawns can also be added to this dish, but even left alone, it's fantastic in every way.

1 Cook the pasta in a pan of boiling water for 2–3 minutes less than the instructions on the packet, until al dente. Tip the pasta into a colander, rinse under cold running water, and drain well. Drizzle ½ teaspoon of olive oil or melted butter on top, then toss and mix thoroughly. This will stop the pasta sticking together.

2 Preheat the oven to 190°C/Fan 170°C/Gas 5. Lightly butter a 3-litre casserole dish.

3 Heat the rapeseed oil in a 30-cm cast-iron frying pan over a medium–high heat, then add the sausage, onion, green and red peppers. Cook, stirring often, until the sausage has begun to brown and the onion and peppers are tender, about 8 minutes. Add the garlic and cook, stirring constantly, for 1 minute. Transfer the sausage mixture to a plate and wipe the frying pan clean.

4 Heat the milk in a medium saucepan over a low–medium heat.

5 In a separate high sided frying pan or large saucepan, melt the butter over a low–medium heat. When the butter bubbles, add the flour. Cook, whisking the butter and flour, for about 1 minute. Once the mixture (roux) has thickened, slowly pour in the hot milk about 60ml at a time, whisking constantly, until the mixture bubbles and becomes a thick sauce. You may have to turn the heat down if the sauce thickens too quickly, use your best judgment.

6 Once the sauce has thickened, remove the pan from the heat. Stir in the salt, Cajun seasoning and, and all but 115–155g of the cheeses. Mix until a smooth sauce forms, then stir in the macaroni. Stir in the peppers, sausage and onion mixture.

7 Transfer the mixture to the baking dish. Sprinkle the remaining cheeses over the top and bake until the cheese has browned, about 30 minutes. Cool for at least 5 minutes, then serve hot.

LASAGNE MAC & CHEESE

COOK TIME: 1 HOUR

SERVES: 4–6

1 x 3-ingredient Mac & Cheese (page 38)

450g minced beef

½ white onion, diced

3 cloves garlic, finely chopped

Non-stick cooking spray or butter, for greasing

370–500ml spaghetti or tomato sauce

115g grated mozzarella cheese

50g grated Parmesan cheese

Basil leaves, to garnish (optional)

This recipe combines a quick and delicious lasagne recipe with a creamy mac and cheese that works well with others! While this recipe uses the 3-ingredient Mac & Cheese, the choice is yours for the base. Other great bases for the Lasagne Mac & Cheese include the Mozzarella Mac & Cheese, Cheese Lover's 5-cheese Mac, Meat Lover's Mac & Cheese, etc. You can't go wrong!

1 Make the 3-ingredient Mac & Cheese (page 38), completing all the steps.

2 Meanwhile, in a separate frying pan, brown the beef, onion, and garlic, stirring occasionally. Drain the mixture and set aside.

3 Preheat the oven to 190°C/Fan 170°C/Gas 5.

4 Lightly spray a 3-litre baking dish with non-stick cooking spray or lightly butter. Spread half of the mac and cheese evenly over the base, then top with a layer of half the meat, then a layer of half the sauce, and finally half of the cheeses. Repeat the layers once more, finishing with the remainder of the cheeses.

5 Bake for 20 minutes. Leave the casserole to rest for 2–3 minutes before serving, garnished with basil, if using.

CHICKEN PARMESAN MAC

COOK TIME: 1 HOUR

SERVES: 4-6

1 x Mozzarella Mac &
   Cheese (page 78) or any
   mac and cheese of your
   choice
450g boneless skinless
   chicken breast, cut into
   2.5–5-cm pieces
1 tbsp finely chopped
   garlic
50g grated Parmesan
   cheese
½ tsp salt
½ tsp freshly ground black
   pepper
½ tsp crushed chilli flakes
   (optional)
Non-stick cooking spray
½ tsp finely chopped
   parsley
55g unsalted butter
1 jar of your favourite
   tomato sauce or
   homemade pasta sauce
50g seasoned Italian
   breadcrumbs
A handful of fresh or dried
   basil leaves (optional)

This dish is a mash-up of two of the best pasta dishes (mac and cheese and chicken Parmesan)! This mac and cheese evokes the mild flavours of the Mozzarella Mac & Cheese with the classic Italian dish. By using Parmesan and tomato sauce, the flavours melt together. If you are an air-fryer household, do not be afraid to use it for the chicken.

1 Make your Mozzarella Mac & Cheese recipe through step 4 (page 78).

2 Preheat the oven to 200°C/Fan 180°C/Gas 6.

3 Toss the chicken pieces in the garlic, 25g of grated Parmesan, salt, black pepper, and chilli flakes. Heat a large frying pan over a medium–high heat with non-stick cooking spray. Once the pan is hot, add the chicken to the pan. Leave untouched for 5 minutes before flipping. Cook for another 2 minutes, then reduce the heat to low.

4 Once the chicken has finished cooking, add the pasta and cheese sauce from your Mozzarella Mac & Cheese to the pan. Stir until everything is evenly mixed. If the cheese is a little stringy, you can stir in a few tablespoons of milk or water, working everything together over a low heat.

5 Melt the butter for the crispy topping for 5–10 seconds, or until it's mostly melted.

6 Tip the pasta mixture into a 3-litre casserole dish. Dollop all over with the pasta sauce. In a medium bowl, toss the melted butter with the breadcrumbs and remaining Parmesan and sprinkle all over the mac and cheese. Bake until browned and bubbly, about 30 minutes. Sprinkle with fresh or dried basil, if you like.

MONTICELLO MAC & CHEESE

COOK TIME: 1 HOUR
SERVES: 4-6

450g macaroni (elbows, or another short shape)

Butter, for greasing

4-5 large celery sticks, diced

225-350g white or chestnut mushrooms, sliced

450g two of the following grated cheeses: Emmental, mozzarella, Gruyère, manchego, Roquefort, Camembert

450g American or Cheddar cheese cut into 2.5-5-cm pieces

50g seasoned or unseasoned breadcrumbs

3 eggs

500ml semi-skimmed or whole milk

½ tsp smoked paprika

1 tsp salt

½ tsp freshly grated black pepper

Pinch of cayenne pepper

Before he became President, Thomas Jefferson spent about four years as US Ambassador to France. In addition to his diplomatic duties, Jefferson used the opportunity to study French food, wine, and agriculture. Jefferson specifically brought with him James Hemings, one of his slaves, to learn French cooking. The two made an agreement that if Hemings would become an expert chef and then train another slave when the two returned to the United States, Jefferson would free him.

Macaroni and cheese was one of the dishes Hemings learned to make and, more importantly, to perfect. While no copies of the recipe Hemings used exist today, historians believe that the recipe in *The Virginia Housewife* by Jefferson's cousin, Mary Randolph, is probably close. While celery and chestnut mushrooms seem less that traditional for a mac and cheese, give it a go, and taste a piece of history.

1 Preheat the oven to 230°C/Fan 210°C/Gas 8.

2 Cook the macaroni in a pan of boiling water for 2-3 minutes less than the instructions on the packet, until al dente. Tip into a colander and drain well.

3 Butter a large casserole dish and make three layers, with each layer made up of pasta, celery, and mushrooms, then sprinkle with cheese. Repeat the layers two more times. After making your three layers, cover the top with breadcrumbs.

4 Beat the eggs with a fork, then add the milk and spices and beat a bit more. Pour the mixture over the mac and cheese and put it into the oven. Reduce the heat to 200°C/Fan 180°C/Gas 6 and bake for 45 minutes to 1 hour until the cheese is bubbling.

TRUFFLE MAC & CHEESE

COOK TIME: 35 MINUTES

SERVES: 4-6

450g elbow macaroni
  or cavatappi

½ tsp olive oil or melted
  butter

115g unsalted butter,
  plus extra for greasing

1.2 litres semi-skimmed
  or whole milk

60g plain flour

2 tsp salt

¼ tsp freshly ground black
  pepper

2 tbsp truffle oil

½ tsp mustard

½ tsp paprika

500g grated mature white
  Cheddar cheese

250g grated Gruyère
  cheese

1 bag (350g) garlic butter
  croutons

Chopped parsley, to
  garnish (optional)

A traditional mac and cheese is one of the most comforting foods in existence. This mac recipe reaches a new level by adding a drizzle of truffle oil, which makes it perfect for a dinner party to show off your culinary prowess. This recipe is also amazing as mac and cheese muffins if baked in muffin tins. If you use mini muffin tins, you have an amazing hors d'oeuvre.

1 Cook the macaroni in a pan of boiling water for 2–3 minutes less than the dinstructions on the packet, until al dente. Tip the macaroni into a colander, rinse under cold running water, and drain well. Drizzle ½ teaspoon of olive oil or melted butter on top, then toss and mix thoroughly. This will stop the pasta sticking together.

2 Preheat the oven to 190°C/Fan 170°C/Gas 5. Lightly butter a 3-litre casserole dish.

3 Heat the milk in a medium saucepan over a low–medium heat.

4 In a separate high-sided frying pan or large saucepan, melt the butter over a low–medium heat. When the butter bubbles, add the flour. Cook, whisking the butter and flour, for about 1 minute. Once the mixture (roux) has thickened, slowly pour in the hot milk about 60ml at a time, whisking constantly, until the mixture bubbles and becomes a thick sauce. You may have to turn the heat down if the sauce thickens too quickly, use your best judgment.

5 Once the sauce has thickened, remove the pan from the heat. Stir in the salt, black pepper, truffle oil, mustard, paprika, and all but 115–155g of the white Cheddar cheese and all the Gruyère. Mix until a smooth sauce forms, then stir in the macaroni.

6 Transfer the mixture to the baking dish. Pulse the croutons in a food processor to make breadcrumbs. Sprinkle the remaining Cheddar cheese and the breadcrumbs over the top. Bake until the cheese has browned, about 30 minutes. Cool for at least 5 minutes, top with parsley, if using, then serve hot.

CHILLI MAC & CHEESE

COOK TIME: 35 MINUTES

SERVES: 4-6

1 tbsp olive oil

4 cloves garlic, finely chopped

1 onion, finely chopped

1 red pepper, deseeded and chopped

450g lean minced beef

2 x 800-g cans chopped tomatoes

2 x 400-g cans red kidney beans, drained

1 litre beef stock (chicken stock will do)

450g elbow macaroni

400g grated cheese (Cheddar, Cheddar with chilli – any tasty cheese), plus extra for sprinkling (optional)

Salt and freshly ground black pepper, to taste

10g finely chopped fresh coriander, to garnish (optional)

Cayenne or chilli powder, for sprinling (optional)

A homemade chilli with the addition of macaroni and cheese = Chilli Mac & Cheese! This is not only comforting, but also makes a fabulous (and quick!) one-pot meal. The secret to this recipe is to turn off the hob as soon as the pasta is just cooked – it will keep cooking in the residual heat. This is a great recipe for using up leftover chilli, or for making from scratch for a barbecue or bring-a-dish party – or why not try it as a contender at your next chilli cookoff?

1 Heat the oil in a large saucepan over a high heat. Add the garlic and onion and cook for 1 minute. Then add the red pepper and cook until the onion is translucent. Add the minced beef and cook, breaking it up as you go.

2 Once the beef has browned, add all the remaining ingredients, except the cheese. Stir, bring to simmer, then turn the heat down to medium. Cover and cook for 10–12 minutes until the macaroni is al dente. Turn off the heat but leave the pan on the hob. Stir through half the cheese – it should be a bit saucy. Adjust salt and pepper to taste. Top with the remaining cheese, put the lid back on and leave until the cheese melts, about 2 minutes (the sauce will absorb the cheese further during this period).

3 Sprinkle with coriander, extra grated cheese and cayenne, if you like, and serve immediately.

MOZZARELLA MAC & CHEESE (CAPRESE)

COOK TIME: 45 MINUTES

SERVES: 4–6

450g cavatappi or similar short-cut pasta

Coarse sea salt and freshly ground black pepper, to taste

115g unsalted butter

60g plain flour

1.5 litres semi-skimmed or whole milk, at room temperature

165g grated mozzarella

115g grated Swiss or Gruyère cheese

70g grated Parmesan

Mozzarella is one of those extremely versatile cheeses. You can use it to top a pasta bake or a pizza, add it to a salad to 'dress it up', and in this case it makes a lovely sauce for a macaroni and cheese. This recipe is less than ordinary and also makes an amazing base for the Chicken Parmesan Mac, the Pizza Mac Bake, and as a Caprese Mac & Cheese (see opposite).

1 Place an oven rack in the middle position of the oven then preheat the oven to 190°C/Fan 170°C/Gas 5.

2 Cook the pasta in a pan of salted boiling water for 2 minutes less than the instructions on the packet, until al dente. Tip into a colander, rinse under cold running water, and drain well.

3 In the same pan, melt the butter over a medium–high heat, then stir in the flour and cook for about a minute, whisking until smooth. Add the milk, a splash or 60ml-ish at a time, whisking or stirring with a wooden spoon after each addition, cooking until thickened. Add the mozzarella, Swiss or Gruyère and 50g Parmesan and stir until melted. Season the sauce with salt and pepper to taste, then stir in the pasta. The sauce should be the perfect amount – it might seem too saucy, but it will thicken in the oven.

Option #1: This option will give you a mac and cheese that really highlights and plays with Italian flavours!

115g shop-bought pizza sauce

40g seasoned panko breadcrumbs or Italian seasoning croutons

2 cloves garlic, finely chopped

½ tsp crushed chilli flakes

Extra-virgin olive oil, for drizzling

A handful of fresh or dried basil leaves (optional)

Option #2: This option is a play on a Caprese Salad. It features fresh mozzarella, sliced Roma tomatoes, and dried basil leaves

2 Roma tomatoes, sliced

225–450g fresh mozzarella cut into slices, or even globs

Balsamic vinegar (optional)

A handful of fresh or dried basil leaves

4 To assemble, you can choose from either version:

OPTION 1

Pour the mixture into a 3-litre casserole dish. Dollop all over with the pizza sauce. In a medium bowl, toss the breadcrumbs, garlic, chilli flakes and remaining the 25g Parmesan with a drizzle of olive oil and sprinkle all over the mac and cheese. Bake until browned and bubbly, about 30 minutes. Sprinkle with basil (if using).

Or:

OPTION 2

Pour into a 3-litre casserole dish and bake as above. Top with the sliced tomatoes, mozzarella, and balsamic after removing from the oven. Sprinkle with fresh or dried basil and enjoy!

JALAPEÑO PEPPER MAC & CHEESE

COOK TIME: 1 HOUR
SERVES: 4-6

450g dried short pasta (cavatappi, elbow, rotini, penne, etc.)

½ tsp olive oil or melted butter

1 tsp olive oil

2–3 fresh jalapeño chillies, deseeded and diced

About ½ small brown onion, diced

3 cloves garlic, finely chopped

This is one of the most fun mash-ups in the book. If you are a fan of jalapeño chillies and love the comfort of mac and cheese, this is for you. The Jalapeño Pepper Mac & Cheese has every great feature of spicy jalapeño chillies, plus comforting and rich mac and cheese. It's a culinary match made in heaven! If you're looking to turn this recipe from a main meal into a starter – or are just looking for great party food – why not consider filling cored jalapeño chillies with this spice-infused mac and cheese?

1 Cook the pasta in a pan of boiling water for 2–3 minutes less than the instructions on the packet, until al dente. Tip the pasta into a colander, rinse under cold running water, and drain well. Drizzle ½ teaspoon of olive oil or melted butter on top, then toss and mix thoroughly. This will stop the pasta sticking together.

625ml whole milk

55g unsalted butter, plus extra for greasing

80g plain flour

840g double cream (optional)

300g cream cheese, softened and cubed

600g grated mozzarella cheese

400g grated or diced mild Cheddar or American cheese

2 tsp coarse sea salt

1 tsp freshly ground black pepper

1 tsp ground cumin

40g panko breadcrumbs

Pickled jalapeño chillies, to garnish

2 Preheat the oven to 190°C/Fan 170°C/Gas 5.

3 In a large pan, heat the 1 teaspoon of olive oil over a medium heat and cook the jalapeños and onion for 2 minutes. Add the garlic and cook for 1 minute, stirring often. Spoon the mixture into a bowl and set aside.

4 Heat the milk in the same pan over a low–medium heat.

5 In a separate high-sided frying pan or large saucepan, melt the butter over a low–medium heat. When the butter bubbles, add the flour. Cook, whisking the butter and flour for about 1 minute. Once the mixture (roux) has thickened, slowly pour in the hot milk about 60ml at a time, whisking constantly, until the mixture bubbles and becomes a thick sauce. You may have to turn the heat down if the sauce thickens too quickly, use your best judgment.

6 Once the sauce has thickened, remove the pan from the heat. Stir in the cream, if using, and mix until a smooth sauce forms. Once smooth, add the cream cheese and stir until it has melted into the sauce. Add most of the mozzarella and Cheddar cheese, setting 250g aside, and stir until it's all melted. Stir in the salt, pepper, cumin, and the jalapeño mixture. If you notice the sauce getting TOO thick, add in a splash of milk and stir. Stir the macaroni into the reserved cheese sauce.

7 Lightly grease a large baking dish, then pour the mixture in. Sprinkle with the remaining cheese and top with the breadcrumbs. Bake until the cheese has browned or become golden on top, about 30 minutes. Allow to cool for at least 5 minutes, then serve garnished with pickled jalapeños. Alternatively, fill cored jalapeños.

MAC & CARBONARA

COOK TIME: 45 MINUTES
SERVES: 4–6

450g pasta shells or cavatappi

Salt

225g thick-cut peppered bacon, diced

2 tbsp plain flour

500ml whole milk

2 large eggs, slightly beaten

115g grated mature Cheddar cheese

100g grated Parmesan cheese

½ tsp grated nutmeg

1 tsp coarse sea salt

½ tsp freshly ground black pepper

Carbonara is a rich Italian pasta dish that consists of a sauce made from egg and Parmesan cheese, usually with the addition of bacon or pancetta and black pepper. This mac and cheese includes peppered thick-cut bacon along with Cheddar and Parmesan cheeses. Serve this creamy pasta with a side salad and crispy garlic bread. You can also fry an egg and throw it on top of these mac and cheese leftovers for a hearty breakfast.

1 Cook the pasta in a large pan of boiling salted water, according to the instructions on the packet. Drain and set aside in a separate large bowl or dish.

2 Return the pasta pan to the hob over a medium heat. Add the bacon and cook for about 10 minutes until it is crispy. Remove the bacon from the pan and drain on kitchen paper. Remove all but 2 tablespoons of the bacon grease from the pan.

3 Sprinkle the flour into the pan with the bacon grease and whisk to combine. Continue to whisk and cook the roux for 1 minute. While whisking, slowly pour in the milk, splash by splash (about 1 tablespoon at a time, and no more than 60ml at a time). As you are cooking the roux, scrape the bottom of the pan to remove any stuck-on bits. Continue to cook, while whisking, for 3–5 minutes until the sauce starts to thicken. Add a few splashes of milk if the sauce seems too thick.

This can also be made as a baked mac, just undercook the pasta and bake at 180°C/Fan 160°C/Gas 4 for 20–30 minutes.

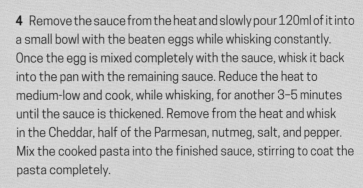

4 Remove the sauce from the heat and slowly pour 120ml of it into a small bowl with the beaten eggs while whisking constantly. Once the egg is mixed completely with the sauce, whisk it back into the pan with the remaining sauce. Reduce the heat to medium-low and cook, while whisking, for another 3–5 minutes until the sauce is thickened. Remove from the heat and whisk in the Cheddar, half of the Parmesan, nutmeg, salt, and pepper. Mix the cooked pasta into the finished sauce, stirring to coat the pasta completely.

5 Pour the finished pasta into a serving dish and sprinkle with the remaining Parmesan and crispy bacon pieces.

PESTO MAC & CHEESE

COOK TIME: 30 MINUTES
SERVES: 4-6

450g penne or elbow
  macaroni
½ tsp olive oil or melted
  butter
1.2 litres whole milk
115g unsalted butter
60g plain flour
2 tsp salt
¼ tsp freshly ground black
  pepper
¼ tsp garlic powder
500g grated Havarti
  cheese
125g grated Pecorino
  Romano, or 220g grated
  mozzarella cheese
4 tbsp pesto
Fresh basil leaves, to
  garnish (optional)

When most people think of pesto, they think of basil pesto, but pesto is just a style of sauce, and it can be made with nearly any herb or vegetable. Spinach and basil are the most common bases for pesto, but it can also be made with sun-dried tomatoes, peppers, and even mushrooms. This recipe uses homemade (or shop-bought) pesto. You can substitute a handful of basil and put it into a food processor in a pinch. It's a unique take on a mac and cheese that is one-part traditional pasta dish and one-part comfort food!

1 Cook the macaroni in a pan of boiling water for 2–3 minutes less than the instructions on the packet, until al dente. Tip the macaroni into a colander, rinse under cold running water, and drain well. Drizzle ½ teaspoon of olive oil or melted butter on top, then toss and mix thoroughly. This will stop the pasta sticking together.

2 Heat the milk in a medium saucepan over a low–medium heat.

3 In a separate high-sided frying pan or large saucepan, melt the butter over a low–medium heat. When the butter bubbles, add the flour. Cook, whisking the butter and flour, for about 1 minute. Once the mixture (roux) has thickened, slowly pour in the hot milk about 60ml at a time, whisking constantly, until the mixture bubbles and becomes a thick sauce. You may have to turn the heat down if the sauce thickens too quickly, use your best judgment.

4 Once the sauce has thickened, remove the pan from the heat. Stir in the salt, black pepper, garlic, and all the cheese. Mix until a smooth sauce forms, then add the pesto and mix until combined. Stir the macaroni into the cheese sauce, then cook on low for a few minutes to thicken the sauce. Serve hot with basil, if using.

Homemade Pesto

COOK TIME: 15 MINUTES
MAKES: ABOUT 250ML

80g fresh basil leaves or baby spinach
45g pine nuts or walnuts
4 cloves garlic, finely chopped (about 1 tbsp)
55g freshly grated Pecorino Romano or Parmesan cheese
120ml extra virgin olive oil
¼ tsp salt, or to taste
⅛ tsp freshly ground black pepper, or to taste

Great for a mac and cheese, pasta, dip for pitta, or sandwich spread, this pesto recipe is extremely versatile. Traditionally, pesto recipes use basil and pine nuts; however, baby spinach can be swapped for basil, and walnuts can be swapped for pine nuts, if you like.

1 In a food processor, pulse the basil (or spinach) and pine nuts (or walnuts) about five times. Add the garlic and cheese and pulse five more times, scraping down the sides of the food processor with a rubber spatula.

2 While the food processor is running, slowly add the olive oil in a steady small stream. Do not add too much or it will emulsify. Add the salt and black pepper to taste.

SKILLET CHEESEBURGER MAC

COOK TIME: 1 HOUR
SERVES: 4-6

450g elbow or pipe
macaroni
1 tsp olive oil
450g minced beef
1 onion, chopped, or 2 tsp
onion powder
3-4 cloves garlic, finely
chopped, or 2 tsp garlic
powder
1 jar (425g) tomato sauce
(or homemade)
240ml whole milk
1 tsp salt, or more to taste
½ tsp freshly ground black
pepper
1 tsp sugar
345g grated Cheddar
cheese

This dish evokes the best parts of minced beef mixed with mac and cheese to make a cheeseburger mac and cheese that's a fan favourite among kids. Feel free to top with ketchup, mustard, and all of your favourite hamburger toppings (including a bun).

1 Cook the macaroni in a pan of boiling water following the instructions on the packet, until al dente. Tip the macaroni into a colander, rinse under cold running water, and drain well.

2 Heat a large frying pan over a medium–high heat. Add the minced beef and cook, breaking up the meat, until nearly fully cooked through, about 3 minutes. Add the onion and garlic and cook for another 2 minutes until they are fragrant and softened. Drain any excess fat if needed.

3 Add the tomato sauce, milk, salt, pepper, and sugar. Over a low heat, bring the mixture to a soft simmer for about 3 minutes, allowing the flavours to combine. Fold in the macaroni, then add the cheese a little at a time until everything combines and the cheese melts and is fully incorporated. Plate up, top with any of your favourite burger toppings, and serve hot.

This mac and cheese/cheeseburger mash-up is sure to be an instant kid favourite!

FANCY MAC & CHEESE

COOK TIME: 1 HOUR
SERVES: 4-6

450g cavatappi
½ tsp olive oil or melted butter
115g unsalted butter, plus extra for greasing
1.2 litres whole milk
60g plain flour
2 tsp salt
¼ tsp freshly ground black pepper
¼ tsp freshly grated nutmeg
¼ tsp garlic powder
¼ tsp mustard powder
250g grated 5-year aged mature Cheddar cheese or 125g Asiago
125g grated fontina cheese
250g grated Gruyère cheese
1 bag (350g) garlic butter croutons (or use leftover bread, see note)

Mac and cheese isn't usually one of those things that is considered luxurious, but this recipe is. It just tastes decadent – and it certainly is! The best pasta for this is the cavatappi pasta; something about this squiggly shape and how it works with the sauce makes a winning combination. The real stars, however, are the cheeses. This recipe uses aged Cheddar, Asiago, Gruyère, and fontina to create a truly magical cheese sauce. Baking this with the croutons is really the special finishing touch.

1 Cook the pasta in a pan of boiling water for 2–3 minutes less than the instructions on the packet, until al dente. Tip the pasta into a colander, rinse under cold running water, and drain well. Drizzle ½ teaspoon of olive oil or melted butter on top, then toss and mix thoroughly. This will stop the pasta sticking together.

2 Preheat the oven to 190°C/Fan 170°C/Gas 5. Lightly butter a 3-litre casserole dish.

3 Heat the milk in a medium saucepan over a low–medium heat.

4 In a separate high-sided frying pan or large saucepan, melt the butter over a low–medium heat. When the butter bubbles, add the flour. Cook, whisking the butter and flour for about 1 minute. Once the mixture (roux) has thickened, slowly pour in the hot milk about 60ml at a time, whisking constantly, until the mixture bubbles and becomes a thick sauce. You may have to turn the heat down if the sauce thickens too quickly, use your best judgment.

continues overleaf

5 Once the sauce has thickened, remove the pan from heat. Stir in the salt, black pepper, nutmeg, garlic and mustard powders, the fontina and Gruyere cheeses, and all but 115g of the aged Cheddar cheese (or all but 25g Asiago). Mix until a smooth cheese sauce forms, then set aside. Stir the drained pasta into the cheese sauce.

6 Pour the mixture into the casserold dish. Pulse the croutons in a food processor to breadcrumbs. Sprinkle the remaining aged Cheddar or Asiago cheese and breadcrumbs over the top. Bake until the cheese has browned, about 30 minutes. Transfer the dish to a wire rack to cool for at least 5 minutes, then serve hot.

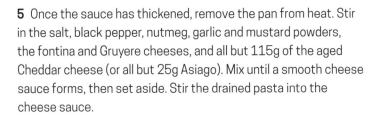

If you don't have any croutons, you can use leftover bread. Just cut into 2.5–5-cm pieces, lightly toss in butter, and toast on a baking sheet in the oven preheated to 180°C/Fan 160°C/Gas 6, for 10 minutes.

LOBSTER MAC & CHEESE

COOK TIME: 1 HOUR

SERVES: 4–6

450g elbow macaroni or cavatappi

½ tsp olive oil or melted butter

115g unsalted butter, plus extra for greasing

1.2 litres semi-skimmed or whole milk

60g plain flour

2 tsp salt

¼ tsp freshly ground black pepper

¼ tsp coarse mustard

¼ tsp garlic powder

¼ tsp onion powder

¼ tsp Old Bay seasoning

385g grated Gruyère cheese

225g cooked lobster (canned lobster can be used, fresh is preferred)

1 bag (350g) garlic butter croutons

125g grated Pecorino Romano cheese

Craving comfort food with a fancy twist? This is the perfect meal for Valentine's Day dinner, an anniversary, or any special occasion. It's sure to wow your guests with its extra-creamy sauce, buttery breadcrumbs, and lavish lobster meat. The best part is that this meal comes together in less than an hour but tastes like it was expertly made at your local restaurant. This dish does use pre-cooked lobster – if you don't live on the coast and aren't lucky enough to easily get fresh lobster at your local fish market, try the seafood counter of your local supermarket, where you may be able to purchase it pre-cooked.

1 Cook the macaroni in a pan of boiling water for 2–3 minutes less than the instructions on the packet, until al dente. Tip the macaroni into a colander, rinse under cold running water, and drain well. Drizzle ½ teaspoon of olive oil or melted butter on top, then toss and mix thoroughly. This will stop the pasta sticking together.

2 Preheat the oven to 190°C/Fan 170°C/Gas 5. Lightly butter a 3-litre casserole dish.

3 Heat the milk in a medium saucepan over a low–medium heat.

4 In a separate high-sided frying pan or large saucepan, melt the butter over a low–medium heat. When the butter bubbles, add the flour. Cook, whisking the butter and flour, for about 1 minute. Once the mixture (roux) has thickened, slowly pour in the hot milk about 60ml at a time, whisking constantly, until the mixture bubbles and becomes a thick sauce. You may have to turn the heat down if the sauce thickens too quickly, use your best judgment.

continues overleaf

LOBSTER MAC & CHEESE

5 Once the sauce has thickened, remove the pan from the heat. Stir in the salt, black pepper, mustard, garlic and onion powders, Old Bay seasoning, and all but 110g of the Gruyère. Mix until a smooth sauce forms, then stir in the macaroni. Carefully stir through the pre-cooked lobster.

6 Pour the mixture into the casserole dish. Pulse the croutons in a food processor to breadcrumbs. Sprinkle the remaining Gruyère, the Parmesan, and breadcrumbs over the top. Bake until the cheese has browned, about 30 minutes. Cool for at least 5 minutes, then serve hot.

PUMPKIN MAC & CHEESE

COOK TIME: 45 MINUTES
SERVES: 4-6

450g elbow macaroni
½ tsp olive oil or melted butter
115g unsalted butter, plus extra for greasing
1 litre semi-skimmed or whole milk
1½ x 425-g cans puréed pumpkin
60g plain flour
2 tsp salt
¼ tsp freshly ground black pepper
1½ tsp chopped thyme
525g grated mature Cheddar cheese
250g grated Gouda

This mac and cheese recipe will be your go-to once summer ends and the leaves start to change colour. Not only is this an easy recipe, this is also the perfect side dish for all of your holiday gatherings. Pair with a nice Chardonnay for an elevated course or just a relaxing weeknight dinner.

1 Cook the macaroni in a pan of boiling water for 2–3 minutes less than the instructions on the packet, until al dente. Tip the macaroni into a colander, rinse under cold running water, and drain well. Drizzle ½ teaspoon of olive oil or melted butter on top, then toss and mix thoroughly. This will stop the pasta sticking together.

2 Preheat the oven to 190°C/Fan 170°C/Gas 5. Lightly butter a 3-litre baking dish. Stir the milk and pumpkin purée together in a small bowl. Heat the milk/pumpkin mix in a medium saucepan over a low–medium heat.

3 In a separate high-sided frying pan or large saucepan, melt the butter over a low–medium heat. When the butter bubbles, add the flour. Cook, whisking the butter and flour, for about 1 minute. Once the mixture (roux) has thickened, slowly pour in the hot milk/pumpkin purée mix, about 60ml at a time, whisking constantly, until the mixture bubbles and becomes a thick sauce. You may have to turn the heat down if the sauce thickens too quickly.

4 Once the sauce has thickened, remove the pan from the heat. Stir in the salt, black pepper, thyme, and all but 115–155g of the Cheddar. Mix until a smooth sauce forms, then stir in the macaroni.

5 Transfer the mixture to the baking dish. Sprinkle the Gouda and remaining Cheddar over the top. Bake until the cheese has browned, about 30 minutes. Cool for 5 minutes, then serve hot.

BACON & BLUE CHEESE MAC

COOK TIME: 1 HOUR
SERVES: 4–6

450g elbow macaroni

½ tsp olive oil or melted butter

115g unsalted butter, plus extra for greasing

1.2 litres semi-skimmed or whole milk

115g plain flour

225g fresh blue cheese

2 tsp salt

225g cooked bacon, chopped

1 bag (350g) garlic butter croutons

11g snipped chives or finely chopped salad or spring onions

The tangy flavour of blue cheese and the savoury taste of bacon make this mac and cheese a tried and true original. This is a great main dish for the blue-cheese lover in your life, and also makes a delicious starter if baked in mini muffin tin (page 19).

1 Cook the macaroni in a pan of boiling water for 2–3 minutes less than the instructions on the packet, until al dente. Tip the macaroni into a colander, rinse under cold running water, and drain well. Drizzle ½ teaspoon of olive oil or melted butter on top, then toss and mix thoroughly. This will stop the pasta sticking together.

2 Preheat the oven to 190°C/Fan 170°C/Gas 5. Lightly butter a 3-litre casserole dish.

3 Heat the milk in a medium saucepan over a low–medium heat.

4 In a separate high-sided frying pan or large saucepan, melt the butter over a low–medium heat. When the butter bubbles, add the flour. Cook, whisking the butter and flour, for about 1 minute. Once the mixture (roux) has thickened, slowly pour in the hot milk about 60ml at a time, whisking constantly, until the mixture bubbles and becomes a thick sauce. You may have to turn the heat down if the sauce thickens too quickly, use your best judgment.

5 Once the sauce has thickened, remove the pan from the heat and stir in the blue cheese, followed by the salt (to blend the flavours). Mix until a smooth sauce forms, then stir in the macaroni. Stir through the chopped bacon.

6 Transfer the mixture to the casserole dish. Pulse the croutons in a food processor to breadcrumbs. Sprinkle the chives or spring onions and breadcrumbs over the top. Bake until the cheese has browned, about 30 minutes. Cool for at least 5 minutes, then serve hot.

PHILLY (MAC &) CHEESE STEAK

COOK TIME: 40 MINUTES

SERVES: 4–6

Non-stick cooking spray

450g large macaroni or cavatappi

450g minced beef

2 brown onions, thinly sliced

2 green peppers, deseeded and thinly sliced

¼ tbsp salt

¼ tbsp freshly ground black pepper

¼ tbsp onion powder

¼ tbsp garlic powder

Pinch of paprika

2 packets cream cheese (450g), cubed

250ml beef stock

115g grated American or Cheddar cheese

115g provolone

Philly Cheese Steak is one of America's favourite hot sandwiches. This recipe uses macaroni, minced beef, green peppers, and a combination of Cheddar or American and provolone cheeses. For those who want to be a little more adventurous, use sliced roast beef deli meat instead of minced beef and top with 2.5-cm pieces of chopped garlic bread and a little butter, finishing with a small sprinkle of provolone, American, or Cheddar cheese.

1 Preheat the oven to 180°C/Fan 160°C/Gas 4. Spray a 3-litre baking dish with non-stick cooking spray.

2 Cook the macaroni in a pan of boiling water following the instructions on the packet, until al dente. Tip the macaroni into a colander, rinse under cold running water, and drain well.

3 In a large frying pan, cook the minced beef, onions, and peppers with the salt, pepper, onion and garlic powders, and paprika over a medium–high heat for 9–11 minutes, stirring occasionally, until the beef is thoroughly cooked and the vegetables are tender – do not drain. Remove from the heat. Stir in the cream cheese until melted. Stir in the hot macaroni and stock.

4 Transfer the macaroni mixture to the baking dish and top with the American or Cheddar cheese and the provolone. Cover with foil and bake for 20–25 minutes until the mixture is hot (at least 73°C in the centre) and the cheese is melted.

VEGAS-STYLE MAC & CHEESE

COOK TIME: 45-50 MINUTES

SERVES: 4-6

450g cavatappi or thicker pasta

½ tsp olive oil or melted butter

Butter, for greasing

55g grated Cheddar cheese

10g breadcrumbs, to garnish (optional)

1 chive, snipped, to garnish (optional)

FOR THE MONEY SAUCE

1 litre whole milk

6 tbsp unsalted butter

60g plain flour

115g cream cheese

115g grated Parmesan cheese

115g grated mature Cheddar cheese

115g grated mild Cheddar cheese

¼ tsp paprika

1-2 tbsp hot sauce (or to taste, depending on how spicy you like your food)

1 tbsp Dijon or brown mustard

Coarse sea salt and freshly ground black pepper, to taste

This mac and cheese boasts a decadent sauce, known affectionately as the 'Money' sauce. It combines Parmesan, mature Cheddar, and mild Cheddar. To 'up the ante', switch out the mature Cheddar for Gruyère. Be warned that when you serve this, your guests will all ask for the recipe. Feel free to tell them, 'what happens in Vegas, stays in Vegas', and withhold it from them!

1 Cook the pasta in a pan of boiling water for 2-3 minutes less than the instructions on the packet, until al dente. Tip the pasta into a colander, rinse under cold running water, and drain well. Drizzle ½ teaspoon of olive oil or melted butter on top, then toss and mix thoroughly. This will stop the pasta sticking together.

2 Preheat the oven to 190°C/Fan 170°C/Gas 5. Lightly butter a 3-litre casserole dish.

3 For the money sauce: Heat the milk in a medium saucepan over a low-medium heat.

4 Melt the butter in a small saucepan over a medium heat, add the flour, whisking constantly. When the butter and flour are blended completely, about a minute, whisk in the milk, 60ml at a time. Continue whisking until the mixture is thickened. Add the cheeses and stir over a low heat until the cheeses melt and have come together to make a smooth sauce. If it seems too thick, add a few splashes of milk and bring back to full heat if needed. Remove from the heat. Add the paprika and season with hot sauce and mustard. Add salt and pepper to taste.

5 Add the pasta to the sauce and stir together over a medium heat until the pasta is coated. Transfer to the casserole dish. Sprinkle the Cheddar cheese over the top and cook in the oven for 30–35 minutes until the cheese is melted and slightly golden, checking halfway through.

6 Remove from the oven and leave to cool slightly, then, if using, serve sprinkled with the breadcrumbs and chives.

CHICKEN POT PIE MAC & CHEESE

COOK TIME: 1 HOUR
SERVES: 4-6

Non-stick cooking spray
  or 2 tbsp butter, for
  greasing
6 tbsp unsalted butter
100g chopped celery
115g chopped onion
140g chopped carrots
30g plain flour
500ml whole milk
500ml chicken stock
1½ tsp salt
1 tsp freshly ground black
  pepper
1 tsp dried thyme
115g grated mild Cheddar
  cheese
780g shredded cooked
  chicken
140g frozen peas (or use
  more cooked carrots)
450g elbow macaroni,
  cooked
1 x 225g packet Cheddar,
  Swiss, or American
  cheese slices
90g crushed buttery round
  crackers, like Ritz

Chicken, cheese sauce, and crushed buttery crackers are the key to this dish. While savoury biscuits or pie crust are certainly options, the crushed buttered crackers give a nice light topping to the dish while still providing crunch. Adding vegetables, chicken, and a rich cheese sauce makes the combination of the two dishes perfect and will have you wondering why you hadn't thought of it before.

1 Preheat the oven to 180°C/Fan 160°C/Gas 4. Spray a 3-litre baking dish with non-stick cooking spray or lightly butter.

2 In a casserole dish or large saucepan, melt the butter over a medium heat. Add the celery, onion, and carrots and cook, stirring occasionally, until softened, about 7 minutes. Add the flour and cook, whisking constantly, for 1 minute. Whisk in the milk, stock, salt, pepper, and thyme. Bring to the boil over a medium–high heat, whisking constantly. Reduce the heat to medium–low and cook, whisking constantly, until the mixture has thickened, about 3 minutes. Remove from the heat.

3 Stir in the cheese until melted. Add the shredded chicken, peas or cooked carrots, and cooked pasta. Mix well until combined. Transfer to the baking dish, top with the cheese slices and sprinkle evenly with the crushed crackers. Bake for 20–25 minutes until bubbly and the cheese has melted. Serve hot.

WILD MUSHROOM MAC & CHEESE

COOK TIME: 45 MINUTES
SERVES: 4-6

450g penne or elbow macaroni

½ tsp olive oil or melted butter, plus extra for cooking

12 small shallots, finely chopped

350g wild mushrooms (see intro)

1 tbsp fresh thyme or ½ tbsp dried

Truffle oil, for drizzling (optional)

115g unsalted butter, plus extra for greasing

1.2 litres semi-skimmed or whole milk

60g plain flour

2 tsp salt

¼ tsp freshly ground black pepper

500g grated Gruyère cheese

125g grated Pecorino Romano or Asiago cheese

1 bag (350g) garlic butter croutons

This mac and cheese is a homage to a white Bolognese sauce. For the best results, use a variety of wild mushrooms. I like to use a combo of chestnut, trumpet, oyster, and button, but any and all will do – even boring old white mushrooms. The thyme and shallots will bring your flavours together. Truffle oil is optional in this dish.

1 Cook the macaroni in a pan of boiling water for 2–3 minutes less than the instructions on the packet, until al dente. Tip the macaroni into a colander, rinse under cold running water, and drain well. Drizzle ½ teaspoon of olive oil or melted butter on top, then toss and mix thoroughly. This will stop the pasta sticking together.

2 While you cook the pasta, heat a large casserole dish or pan over a medium–high heat. Add a little olive oil, shallots, mushrooms, and thyme. Cook until the shallots and mushrooms have softened and are beginning to brown. Remove from the heat and drizzle with truffle oil (if using).

3 Preheat the oven to 190°C/Fan 170°C/Gas 5. Lightly butter a 3-litre casserole dish.

4 Heat the milk in a medium saucepan over a low–medium heat.

5 In a separate high-sided frying pan or large saucepan, melt the butter over a low–medium heat. When the butter bubbles, add the flour. Cook, whisking the butter and flour, for about 1 minute. Once the mixture (roux) has thickened, slowly pour in the hot milk about 60ml at a time, whisking constantly, until the mixture bubbles and becomes a thick sauce. You may have to turn the heat down if the sauce thickens too quickly, use your best judgment.

6 Once the sauce has thickened, remove the pan from the heat. Stir in the salt, black pepper, and all but 115–155g Gruyère (and/or 50g Pecorino, if using). Mix until a smooth sauce forms, then stir in the macaroni. Add the mushrooms and shallots.

7 Transfer the mixture to the baking dish. Pulse the croutons in a food processor to breadcrumbs. Sprinkle the remaining cheese and the breadcrumbs over the top. Bake until the cheese has browned, about 30 minutes. Cool for at least 5 minutes, then serve hot.

STUFFED MAC & CHEESE

COOK TIME: 1 HOUR
SERVES: 4–6

500ml milk
500ml cream
225g mild Cheddar or
  American cheese
175g cream cheese, cut
  into small pieces
70g grated Parmesan
  cheese
460g grated mature
  Cheddar cheese
1 tsp dry mustard
¼ tsp paprika
¼ tsp cayenne pepper
½ tsp coarse sea salt

This mac and cheese is the turducken of pasta dishes! It's a double mac and cheese, where a small version of shells are cooked and then spooned into large pasta shells, then baked with more cheese. It's a fun dish that is always a crowd-pleaser. Mix and match your cheeses with what you have on hand. You can also add ham, chicken, or vegetables. This dish is also great to mix and match with mac recipes.

1 Bring the milk and cream to a simmer in a large saucepan over a medium heat. Whisk in the Cheddar or American cheese, cream cheese, and Parmesan until smooth. Remove from the heat and whisk in the Cheddar, mustard, paprika, cayenne, salt, and black pepper. Divide the sauce in half, reserving one half.

1 tsp freshly ground black
  pepper
225g large pasta shells
½ tsp olive oil or melted
  butter
Butter, for greasing
225g small pasta shells
120ml tomato sauce
90g finely crushed cheese
  crackers

2 Cook the large shells in a pan of boiling water for 2–3 minutes less than the instructions on the packet, until al dente. Tip the pasta into a colander, rinse under cold running water, and drain well. Drizzle ½ teaspoon of olive oil or melted butter on top, then toss and mix thoroughly. This will stop the pasta sticking together.

3 Preheat the oven to 190°C/Fan 170°C/Gas 5. Lightly butter a 3-litre casserole dish.

4 Put half the sauce into the baking dish, spreading it into an even layer. Transfer the large pasta shells to the bowl of reserved sauce and toss to coat. Remove to the baking dish.

5 Cook the small shells in the same pan of water according to the packet instructions, as before. Drain well, then transfer to the bowl with the remaining sauce and toss to coat with the sauce.

6 Heat the tomato sauce on the hob or in the microwave.

7 Spoon the small shells into the big shells and line them up neatly in the baking dish, nestling them in the cheese sauce. Sprinkle with the crushed cheese crackers. Drizzle the tomato sauce on top of the large shells and bake until hot through, bubbling, and the crackers are starting to brown, about 15 minutes. Allow to cool for 5 minutes before serving.

MEAT LOVER'S MAC & CHEESE
(THREE LITTLE PIGS MAC)

COOK TIME: 45 MINUTES
SERVES: 4–6

450g elbow macaroni

½ tsp olive oil or melted butter

115g unsalted butter, plus extra for greasing

1.2 litres semi-skimmed or whole milk

115g plain flour

2 tsp salt

¼ tsp freshly ground black pepper

¼ tsp freshly grated nutmeg

¼ tsp garlic powder

Pinch of chipotle chilli powder, or to taste (optional)

500g grated mature and/or mild Cheddar cheese

continues overleaf

With over 450g of meat in it, this Meat Lover's Mac & Cheese is not for the faint of heart. It is jam-packed with everything you crave – and then some. Piled high with melty cheese, crispy bacon, juicy sausage crumbles, and herby Italian seasoning, this recipe will hit the spot, be it a late-night craving, a hangover, or just plain old Monday blues.

1 Cook the macaroni in a pan of boiling water for 2–3 minutes less than the instructions on the packet, until al dente. Tip the macaroni into a colander, rinse under cold running water, and drain well. Drizzle ½ teaspoon of olive oil or melted butter on top, then toss and mix thoroughly. This will stop the pasta sticking together.

2 Preheat the oven to 190°C/Fan 170°C/Gas 5. Lightly butter a 3-litre casserole dish.

3 Heat the milk in a medium saucepan over a low–medium heat.

4 In a separate high-sided frying pan or large saucepan, melt the butter over a low–medium heat. When the butter bubbles, add the flour. Cook, whisking the butter and flour, for about 1 minute. Once the mixture (roux) has thickened, slowly pour in the hot milk about 60ml at a time, whisking constantly, until the mixture bubbles and

continues overleaf

MEAT LOVER'S MAC & CHEESE

250g grated mild Cheddar cheese or 125g grated Pecorino Romano cheese

250g sausage, cooked and sliced or chopped

250g ham, cooked and chopped

250g bacon, cooked and chopped

1 bag (350g) garlic butter croutons (optional)

Sliced chives, to garnish (optional)

becomes a thick sauce. You may have to turn the heat down if the sauce thickens too quickly, use your best judgment.

5 Once the sauce has thickened, remove the pan from the heat. Stir in the salt, black pepper, nutmeg, garlic powder, chipotle chilli, if using, and all but 115–155g Cheddar cheese (or 50g Parmesan, if using). Mix until a smooth sauce forms, then stir in the macaroni. Add the sausage, ham, and bacon.

6 Transfer the mixture to the casserole dish. If using, pulse the croutons in a food processor to breadcrumbs. Sprinkle the remaining Cheddar cheese and breadcrumbs over the top. Bake until the cheese has browned, about 30 minutes. Cool for at least 5 minutes, then serve hot, topped with optional sliced chives.

SRIRACHA & SHRIMP MAC & CHEESE

COOK TIME: 1 HOUR
SERVES: 4-6

450g cavatappi or penne
½ tsp olive oil or melted
 butter, plus extra oil for
 frying
1 tsp grated garlic
 (optional)
1 tsp grated fresh ginger
 (optional)
300g shrimp/prawns,
 peeled and deveined
1.2 litres whole milk
115g unsalted butter
60g plain flour
2 tsp salt
¼ tsp freshly ground black
 pepper
¼ tsp freshly grated
 nutmeg
¼ tsp garlic powder
500g grated Havarti
 cheese
230g grated Gouda
3 tbsp sriracha, or to taste
15g sliced salad or spring
 onions or parsley, to
 garnish

A spicy take on the classic mac and cheese. This recipe mixes it up a little by using cavatappi or penne pasta and Gouda and Havarti cheeses, and adds shrimps to the mix. While most mac and cheeses are usually yellow and lack pizazz, this one is a showstopper with its red hue. The salad onion garnish also gives the colour palette a little bit of extra fun. This recipe is wonderfully unique and sure to be a hit at your next book club or dinner party.

1 Cook the pasta in a pan of boiling water according to the instructions on the packet. Tip the pasta into a colander, rinse under cold running water, and drain well. Once drained, drizzle ½ teaspoon of olive oil or melted butter on top, then toss and mix thoroughly. This will stop the pasta sticking together.

2 While cooking the pasta, start preparing the shrimp/prawns. Heat a pan with a little oil over a medium heat and add the fresh garlic and ginger, if using. Add the shrimp/prawns to the pan for a few minutes, until pink and cooked through. Remove from the heat and set aside.

3 Heat the milk in a separate medium or large saucepan over a low-medium heat.

4 In a high-sided frying pan or large saucepan, melt the butter over a low-medium heat. When the butter bubbles, add the flour. Cook, whisking the butter and flour until brown, about 3 minutes. Once the mixture (roux) has thickened, slowly pour in the hot

continues overleaf

milk about 60ml at a time, whisking constantly, until the mixture bubbles and becomes a thick sauce. You may have to turn the heat down if the sauce thickens too quickly, use your best judgment.

5 Once the sauce has thickened, remove the pan from the heat. Stir in the salt, black pepper, nutmeg, garlic powder, and cheeses. Mix until a smooth sauce forms, then stir in the sriracha, starting with 1 tablespoon and working up to 3 (or your desired level). Tip the cooked macaroni into the cheese sauce in the pan, stir well and cook on low for a few minutes to thicken. Transfer to a serving dish, add the shrimp/prawns, and garnish with the sliced salad or spring onions. Serve hot!

This dish is a real showstopper!

BUTTERMILK & SOURDOUGH
MAC & CHEESE

COOK TIME: 45 MINUTES

SERVES: 4–6

450g elbow macaroni

½ tsp olive oil or melted butter

115g unsalted butter, plus extra for greasing

1.2 litres buttermilk (or buttermilk substitute, see intro)

60g plain flour

2 tsp salt

¼ tsp freshly ground black pepper

¼ tsp garlic powder

¼ tsp onion powder

¼ tsp mustard powder or prepared spicy brown mustard

¼ tsp paprika

500g grated mild Cheddar cheese, plus 115g for sprinkling

Sourdough Bread (page 119), or baguette croutons, chopped into 2.5–5-cm cubes and toasted and 1 bag (350g) garlic butter croutons

Slightly tangy and incredibly rich is the best way to describe this mac and cheese. This recipe calls for a mature Cheddar and savoury sourdough breadcrumbs, which very easily elevate this to another level. If you don't have buttermilk, don't worry, it's an easy ingredient to create – just add 1 tablespoon of vinegar to 250ml milk, wait five minutes and, voila! – buttermilk.

1 Cook the macaroni in a pan of boiling water for 2–3 minutes less than the instructions on the packet, until al dente. Tip the macaroni into a colander, rinse under cold running water, and drain well. Drizzle ½ teaspoon of olive oil or melted butter on top, then toss and mix thoroughly. This will stop the pasta sticking together.

2 Preheat the oven to 190°C/Fan 170°C/Gas 5. Lightly butter a 3-litre casserole dish.

3 Heat the buttermilk in a medium saucepan over a low–medium heat.

4 In a separate high-sided frying pan or large saucepan, melt the butter over a low–medium heat. When the butter bubbles, add the flour. Cook, whisking the butter and flour, for about 1 minute. Once the mixture (roux) has thickened, slowly pour in the warm buttermilk about 60ml at a time, whisking constantly, until the mixture bubbles and becomes a thick sauce. You may have to turn the heat down if the sauce thickens too quickly, use your best judgment.

continues overleaf

BUTTERMILK & SOURDOUGH MAC & CHEESE

5 Once the sauce has thickened, remove the pan from the heat. Stir in the salt, black pepper, garlic, onion and mustard powders, paprika, and all the cheese minus 115g. Mix until a smooth sauce forms, then stir in the macaroni.

6 Transfer the mixture to the baking dish. Pulse the sourdough and croutons in a food processor to breadcrumbs. Sprinkle the cheese and breadcrumbs over the top. Bake until the cheese has browned, about 30 minutes (or bubbly!). Cool for at least 5 minutes, then serve hot.

Easy Sourdough Bread

COOK TIME: 10 HOURS
MAKES: 1 LOAF

450g plain flour, plus extra for
   dusting
2 tsp salt
¾ tsp fast-action dried yeast

370ml lukewarm water
   (40–46°C, no warmer)
1 tbsp garlic powder, Italian
   seasoning, or
   grated cheese
   (optional)

This simple variation of a no-knead bread recipe is the perfect base for homemade croutons, or as a sandwich base for the Simple Mac & Cheese Toastie, Pulled Pork MC Sandwich, or spread with a dollop of fresh pesto and goat's cheese or mozzarella.

1 Place the flour, salt, and yeast in a large bowl and whisk to combine. Make a well in the centre and pour in the water. Stir until it forms a shaggy dough. Cover the dough bowl with cling film or a tea towel and let rise for 6–8 hours at room temperature or in your oven with just the oven light on until it has doubled in size and bubbly.

2 Add any garlic, Italian seasoning, or cheese, if using. Shape the dough, cover again, and let rise for another hour. Lightly flour a piece of baking paper. Turn the dough out onto it, folding the dough over on itself at least once while you do so. Quickly shape the dough into a ball, then cover again and leave to rise for another 1 hour.

3 While the dough rises for that final hour, preheat the oven. About 30 minutes in, arrange a rack in the middle of the oven. Place a large casserole dish with its lid on the rack. Increase the heat of the oven to 230°C/ Fan 210°C/Gas 8.

4 Using the baking paper to carry and transfer the loaf to the casserole dish. If liked, make a slash or shallow cut on the top of the dough with kitchen shears or a sharp knife so that the bread can expand while baking. Using a thick oven glove, cover the pan with the lid and bake for 30 minutes. Uncover and bake for another 15 minutes, or until the centre of the loaf is 110°C.

5 Remove the casserole dish from the oven and use the baking paper to transfer the bread to a wire rack. Cool for at least 15 minutes. Slice the bread and use immediately or leave to stand overnight for croutons or breadcrumbs.

PIZZA MAC BAKE

COOK TIME: 45 MINUTES

SERVES: 4–6

Butter, for greasing

350g macaroni, shells, or cavatappi

½ tsp olive oil or melted butter

350ml evaporated milk

350g grated mild or medium Cheddar cheese

1 can (175–225g) petite diced tomatoes, drained

1 can (175–225g) pizza sauce

1 small green pepper, deseeded and chopped

1 small sweet red pepper, deseeded and chopped

200g grated Italian cheese blend

60g sliced pepperoni

Any other pizza-style toppings of your choice, such as mushrooms, jalapeño chillies, ham, sausage, olives, anchovies – or even pineapple, if the mood takes you

Salt and freshly ground black pepper, to taste

Fresh chives, parsley, or basil, to garnish

If you took a poll, most people would likely list mac and cheese and pizza as their favourite comfort foods. This mac combines both – it includes the toppings for a supreme, fully loaded pizza, but you can also customize your pizza mac around your favourite pizza toppings.

1 Preheat the oven to 190°C/Fan 170°C/Gas 5. Lightly butter a large baking dish.

2 Cook the macaroni in a pan of boiling water for 2–3 minutes less than the instructions on the packet, until al dente. Tip the macaroni into a colander, rinse under cold running water, and drain well. Drizzle ½ teaspoon of olive oil or melted butter on top, then toss and mix thoroughly. This will stop the pasta sticking together.

3 Bring the evaporated milk to the boil in a medium saucepan over a medium-high heat. Add the cheese and immediately reduce the heat to low, whisking constantly until the cheese has melted and the liquid has thickened to a creamy sauce, about 2 minutes. Stir in the macaroni and transfer to the casserole dish.

4 In a small bowl, combine the tomatoes and pizza sauces, then drop spoonfuls over the macaroni. Top with the peppers, Italian cheese, pepperoni, and any other toppings. Bake for 25–30 minutes until bubbly. Add salt and pepper, if needed and garnish with herbs.

The perfect mash-up of two comfort food favourites.

BUFFALO CHICKEN MAC & CHEESE

COOK TIME: 1 HOUR
SERVES: 4–6

450g boneless, skinless chicken breast

175ml blue cheese or Ranch dressing

450g cavatappi, shells, or macaroni

½ tsp olive oil or melted butter

55g unsalted butter

620ml whole milk

60g plain flour

2 tbsp tomato purée

120ml double cream

115g cream cheese, softened and at room temperature

345g grated Cheddar cheese

continues overleaf

For the spicy food lovers out there, this mac and cheese is for you! This dish is a nod to buffalo-style hot wings and incorporates all the best parts about the dish into a mac. Using blue cheese and/or Ranch dressing, Cheddar, and cream cheese along with buffalo sauce (or a homemade version), this dish is sure to be a crowd-pleaser with its mix of spicy and cool flavours.

1 Put the chicken breasts into a saucepan of cold water over a medium heat and gradually bring to the boil. Cook for 15–20 minutes until the chicken is cooked through.

2 Remove the chicken, pour out the water, and let the chicken cool. Once cool, use two forks to shred it. Toss the shredded chicken with the blue cheese or Ranch dressing and set aside.

3 While the chicken is cooking, cook the pasta in a pan of boiling water for 2–3 minutes less than the instructions on the packet, until al dente. Tip the pasta into a colander, rinse under cold running water, and drain well. Drizzle ½ teaspoon of olive oil or melted butter on top, then toss and mix thoroughly. This will stop the pasta sticking together.

4 Heat the milk in a medium saucepan over a low–medium heat.

5 Melt the butter in a large saucepan over a medium heat. Add the flour and stir constantly for 1 minute. Add the tomato purée and stir to incorporate into a thick paste. Add the double cream and milk a few splashes, and no more than 60ml, at a time, stirring constantly with each addition. Cook until the sauce is at a soft boil or starting to thicken into a sauce.

continues overleaf

BUFFALO CHICKEN MAC & CHEESE

120ml Buffalo Sauce (see opposite) or 60ml hot sauce, plus 60ml melted butter
1 tsp mustard powder
½ tsp onion powder
1 tsp salt
1 tsp freshly grated black pepper

6 Turn the heat to low–medium. Add the cream cheese and Cheddar cheese, buffalo sauce or hot sauce and butter, mustard and onion powders, salt, and pepper. Stir to combine and heat through while whisking to fully incorporate the ingredients. Remove from the heat.

7 Stir in the pasta and then the shredded chicken to combine. Serve immediately.

For the spicy food lovers out there, this mac & cheese is for you!

Buffalo Sauce

COOK TIME: 25 MINUTES
MAKES: 250ML

175ml hot pepper sauce (such as Frank's RedHot®)
115g cold unsalted butter
1½ tbsp white vinegar
¼ tsp Worcestershire sauce
¼ tsp cayenne pepper
¼ tsp garlic powder
¼ tsp salt
¼ tsp freshly ground black pepper

There are a few things that are just better when made from scratch, and buffalo sauce is one of them. Buffalo sauce is essentially hot pepper sauce and butter mixed together. While often used to toss over chicken wings and served alongside blue cheese or Ranch dressing and sliced carrots and celery sticks to cool it down, this added to mac and cheese really brings out the flavour of a Cheddar cheese. The flavours pair really well.

1 Combine the hot sauce, butter, vinegar, Worcestershire sauce, cayenne, garlic powder, salt, and pepper in a saucepan over a medium heat. Whisk to combine. Bring to a simmer, whisking occasionally.

2 Simmer for 3–5 minutes, right until it's up to the boil. Remove from the heat and whisk a few times to thoroughly mix the ingredients. Set aside until cooled.

SKILLET BACON PRIMAVERA
MAC & CHEESE

COOK TIME: 45 MINUTES
SERVES: 4–6

450g cavatappi
½ tsp olive oil or melted
  butter
2 large yellow summer
  squash
Non-stick cooking spray or
  butter, for cooking
90g chopped fresh spinach
2 large Roma or Heirloom
  tomatoes, deseeded and
  chopped

Cheese and vegetables! What could be better? This recipe takes a bacon primavera and adds a burst of fresh vegetables to this mac and cheese dish. It's hearty, while still being light. One pro tip is to use Laughing Cow or a soft/spreadable cheese in lieu of the Swiss for a creamier sauce.

1 Cook the pasta in a pan of boiling water for 2–3 minutes less than the instructions on the packet, until al dente. Tip the pasta into a colander, rinse under cold running water, and drain well. Drizzle ½ teaspoon of olive oil or melted butter on top, then toss and mix thoroughly. This will stop the pasta sticking together.

170g grated Swiss cheese

4 tbsp sour cream

4 slices fat-free Cheddar cheese

6 slices of thick, centre-cut bacon, cooked and crumbled or chopped

Salt and freshly ground black pepper, to taste (optional)

Sliced chives, to garnish (optional)

2 While the pasta cooks, cut the squash into pieces similar to the size of penne, about 5cm long and 1cm thick.

3 Spray or butter a large frying pan (with a lid) with non-stick spray and set over a medium heat. Add the squash, cover, and cook for 5–6 minutes, occasionally uncovering to stir. Add the spinach and tomatoes to the pan, cover again, and cook for 1–2 minutes. Uncover and continue to cook, stirring occasionally, until the spinach has wilted, the tomatoes are soft, and all the excess liquid has cooked off, about 3–5 minutes. If needed, drain off any excess liquid. Set aside.

4 Place the Swiss cheese in a microwaveable bowl and add the sour cream and cheese slices. Microwave for 30 seconds, then stir thoroughly. Microwave for another 30 seconds, and repeat until the cheeses have fully melted. Mix until smooth. (This can also be done on the hob in a small pan over a low heat.)

5 Add the cheese mixture and cooked veggies to the pasta and toss to coat. Top with the bacon and if needed, bring to your desired temperature on the hob. If you like, season with salt and pepper to taste and garnish with chives.

A scrumptious combination of bacon, cheese, and vegetables.

OKTOBERFEST MAC & CHEESE

**COOK TIME: 45 MINUTES–
1 HOUR
SERVES: 4–6**

2 bottles of German lager
  beer, such as Augustiner,
  Hacker-Pschorr, Hofbräu,
  Löwenbräu, Paulaner,
  Spaten

50g elbow macaroni or
  cavatappi

½ tsp olive oil or melted
  butter

1.2 litres whole milk

115g unsalted butter

60g plain flour

2 tsp salt

1 tsp freshly ground black
  pepper

2 tsp coarse mustard

1 tsp onion powder

500g grated Gouda or
  mature Cheddar cheese

230g grated smoked
  Cheddar, smoked bacon
  Cheddar, or a smoky
  cheese of your choice

450g Bratwurst, cooked in
  beer and sliced

One thing that many of us can look forward to as summer winds down is celebrating the foods that follow, along with Oktoberfest! Autumn is the perfect time for sausages, pretzels, and beer, and even if you are not in Germany, you can still celebrate with this festive mac and cheese recipe. In a nod to this traditional German festival, this recipe adds Bratwurst, mature Cheddar, and a smoky bacon Cheddar cheese. If you prefer to go baked, undercook the pasta by three minutes, top with toasted soft pretzels as your crust, and bake until bubbly!

1 Pour all the beer, minus 120ml, into a medium saucepan and add the macaroni. Cook over a medium–high heat until the macaroni is tender. Transfer the cooked macaroni to a colander, rinse under cold running water, and drain well. Once drained, drizzle ½ teaspoon of olive oil or melted butter on top and toss and mix thoroughly. This will stop the pasta sticking together.

2 Heat the milk in a medium saucepan over a low–medium heat.

3 In a separate high-sided frying pan or large saucepan, melt the butter over a low–medium heat. When the butter bubbles, add the flour. Cook, whisking the butter and flour for about 1 minute. Once the mixture (roux) has thickened, slowly pour in the hot milk about 60ml at a time, whisking constantly, until the mixture bubbles and becomes a thick sauce. You may have to turn the heat down if the sauce thickens too quickly, use your best judgment.

4 Once the sauce has thickened, remove the pan from the heat. Stir in the salt, black pepper, mustard, and onion powder. Add all the cheeses (and sausage at this point, if preferred) and mix until a smooth sauce forms, then stir the reserved beer and cooked macaroni into the cheese sauce. Mix and cook on low for a few minutes to thicken the sauce. Leave to stand for about 10 minutes, before serving, it will thicken as it cools. (Alternatively, add the sliced sausage as a topping.)

Recipes

The Second Stage

BREAKFAST MAC & CHEESE

COOK TIME: 45 MINUTES-
   1 HOUR
SERVES: 4-6

450g shells or elbow
   macaroni

½ tsp olive oil or melted
   butter

115g unsalted butter, plus
   extra for greasing

450g breakfast sausage,
   removed from casings
   and crumbled (or bacon)

1 large onion, diced

1 red pepper, deseeded
   and diced

1 jalapeño chilli, deseeded
   and diced

¼ tsp garlic powder

1 litre whole or semi-
   skimmed milk

60g plain flour

2 tsp salt

¼ tsp freshly ground black
   pepper

¼ tsp freshly grated
   nutmeg

Pinch (or to taste) of
   cayenne pepper or
   chipotle chilli powder
   (optional)

500g grated Gouda or
   Cheddar with chilli
   cheese

230g grated mild Cheddar
   cheese or 125g grated
   Pecorino Romano cheese

450g frozen tater tots or
   8-12 frozen hash brown

While mac and cheese isn't a dish we usually consider for breakfast, this recipe will make you wonder why you hadn't tried it before! This delicious and filling dish will give any breakfast fry-up or loaded omelette a run for its money. This mac has cheese, onion, red pepper, and jalapeño, along with crispy tater tots or hash browns, which mix perfectly with Gouda or Cheddar with chilli cheese and breakfast sausage. You can even slather it with ketchup, if you so desire!

1 Cook the macaroni in a pan of boiling water for 2–3 minutes less than the instructions on the packet, until al dente. Tip the macaroni into a colander, rinse under cold running water, and drain well. Drizzle ½ teaspoon of olive oil or melted butter on top, then toss and mix thoroughly. This will stop the pasta sticking together.

2 Preheat the oven to 190°C/Fan 170°C/Gas 5. Lightly butter a large baking dish.

3 In a large pan over a medium heat, cook the sausage, breaking it with a wooden spoon as it cooks. Once no longer pink, remove it to a bowl with a slotted spoon and set aside. Add the onion, red pepper, and jalapeño to the same pan and cook for 4–5 minutes until softened. Stir in the garlic powder and spoon the onion mixture into the bowl with the cooked sausage.

4 Heat the milk in the same pan over a low-medium heat.

5 In a separate high-sided frying pan or large saucepan, melt the butter over a low-medium heat. When the butter bubbles, add the flour. Cook, whisking the butter and flour for about 1 minute. Once

continues overleaf

the mixture (roux) has thickened, slowly pour in the hot milk about 60ml at a time, whisking constantly, until the mixture bubbles and becomes a thick sauce. You may have to turn the heat down if the sauce thickens too quickly, use your best judgment.

6 Once the sauce has thickened, remove the pan from the heat and stir in the salt, black pepper, nutmeg, cayenne or chipotle, if using, and all but 115–155g Gouda and Cheddar cheese (or 50g Parmesan, if using). Mix until a smooth cheese sauce forms, then stir in the cooked macaroni. Add the sausage and pepper mixture and stir to combine.

7 Pour the mixture into the baking dish. Sprinkle the remaining Cheddar cheese and the tater tots or hash browns over the top, or serve on the side. Bake until the cheese and tots have browned or become golden, about 30 minutes. Cool for at least 5 minutes, then serve hot.

This delicious and filling dish will give any breakfast fry-up or loaded omelette a run for its money.

MAC & CHEESE WAFFLES

COOK TIME: 20-60 MINUTES

**MAKES 8 WAFFLES
(DEPENDING ON SIZE OF
WAFFLE MAKER)**

450g elbow macaroni

½ tsp olive oil or melted
butter

1.2 litres whole milk

115g unsalted butter

60g plain flour

2 tsp salt

¼ tsp freshly ground black
pepper

¼ tsp freshly grated
nutmeg

¼ tsp garlic powder

Pinch of cayenne pepper or
chipotle chilli powder, or
to taste (optional)

500g grated mature and/or
mild Cheddar cheese

230g grated mild Cheddar
cheese or 125g grated
Pecorino Romano cheese

Non-stick cooking spray

Hot sauce and maple syrup,
to serve

Mac and cheese waffles aren't a dish you will see everywhere, but they sure are delicious! Similar to a hash brown or other smooshed savoury treat, this dish is just as it sounds, mac and cheese baked in a waffle iron. This can then be topped with traditional waffle toppings or used as a more savoury base for a meal. These waffles are also a great choice to serve alongside fried chicken.

1 Cook the macaroni in a pan of boiling water for 2–3 minutes less than the instructions on the packet, until al dente. Tip the macaroni into a colander, rinse under cold running water, and drain well. Drizzle ½ teaspoon of olive oil or melted butter on top, then toss and mix thoroughly. This will stop the pasta sticking together.

2 Heat the milk in a medium saucepan over a low–medium heat.

3 In a separate high-sided frying pan or large saucepan, melt the butter over a low–medium heat. When the butter bubbles, add the flour. Cook, whisking the butter and flour, for about 1 minute.

4 Once the mixture (roux) has thickened, slowly pour in the hot milk about 60ml at a time, whisking constantly, until the mixture bubbles and becomes a thick sauce. You may have to turn the heat down if the sauce thickens too quickly, use your best judgment.

5 Once the sauce has thickened, remove the pan from the heat. Stir in the salt, black pepper, nutmeg, garlic powder, cayenne or chipotle, if using, and all but 115–155g Cheddar cheese (or 50g Parmesan, if using). Mix until a smooth sauce forms, then stir in the macaroni. Mix and cook on low for a few minutes to thicken

continues overleaf

the sauce. Pour the mixture into a baking tray. Cool, then put into the fridge for about 1 hour, or until the mac and cheese has solidified (it can also be frozen at this point).

6 Once solidified and cold, cut into 10 x 10-cm sections. You should get about 8–12 squares. Heat the waffle maker following the manufacturer's instructions. Once ready, spray the waffle maker with non-stick cooking spray and put one of the mac and cheese squares in, sprinkle 1 tablespoon of the reserved cheese on top and top with another of the mac and cheese squares.

7 Place the mac and cheese in the waffle maker. Close and cook until golden brown on both sides and the cheese has crisped up, about 6 minutes. Remove from waffle iron and serve with syrup and hot sauce or other toppings of your choice. Repeat for the remaining waffles.

CUSTOMIZE IT

Top with traditional waffle toppings or use as a savoury base for favourites like fried chicken, pulled pork, or even a fried egg as a breakfast treat.

MAC **MY BURGER**

Mac & Cheese Burger Buns

COOK TIME: 20 MINUTES

MAKES: 12 BUNS

1 x mac and cheese recipe (Perfect Baked, Bacon & Blue Cheese, Southern Mac & Cheese all work well)

300g breadcrumbs or crushed croutons

1 tbsp dried basil

1½ tsp dried oregano

1½ tsp crushed chilli flakes

½ tsp salt

½ tsp freshly ground black pepper

8 eggs

Oil, for deep-frying

It's time to fry up some mac and cheese burger buns! This recipe makes either 12 buns or 12 large fried mac and cheese patties. For those who really love mac and cheese, or for those who enjoy creating decadent dishes, create the ultimate mac and cheese burger by frying these up and using as the bun for a Mac & Cheese Stuffed Burger (page 140).

1 Using a 8–10-cm biscuit cutter, cut out six circles of mac and cheese and cut each circle in half widthways. (You can also pour the mac and cheese into a baking tray when making, for easier portioning). Place on a baking tray, and transfer to the freezer for at least 1 hour.

2 In a medium bowl, mix together the breadcrumbs or croutons, basil, oregano, chilli flakes, salt, and pepper.

3 When you are ready to make the buns, in a separate medium bowl, whisk the eggs well. In a large, deep pan or casserole dish, heat about 8 cm of oil over a medium, steady heat. Start frying when your heat reaches a consistent 180°C.

4 Once the mac and cheese 'buns' are solidified together, working carefully and keeping the other buns cold while you work, carefully dip each mac and cheese bun half into the egg batter to coat, shaking off any excess, then roll in the breadcrumb mixture to coat, then add directly to the hot oil. Fry until golden brown, flipping halfway through. Each side should take about 3 minutes. Transfer to kitchen paper to drain. Serve with the Mac & Cheese Stuffed Burgers (page 140).

Mac & Cheese Stuffed Burgers

COOK TIME: 25 MINUTES
SERVES: 4-6

900g 85% lean minced beef

1 tbsp Worcestershire sauce or steak sauce

3 cloves garlic, finely chopped

¼ tsp salt

½ tsp freshly ground black pepper

1 cup leftover mac and cheese recipe of your choice (such as Bacon & Blue Cheese)

40g grated white Cheddar cheese (or whatever cheese you like)

1 white onion, sliced

6 brioche or pretzel buns (burger buns of your choice, really), sliced in half horizontally

Spicy ketchup or other sauces from this book

Iceberg or Frisée (or Bibb)

Gherkin slices (bread and butter pickles and sweet pickles also work)

This recipe takes leftover mac and cheese and fries it up between two small burger patties, making for a delicious and filling cheese-lovers' burger patty! Bring the meal to the next level by serving these burgers on the Mac & Cheese Burger Buns (page 139). Try this as a once in a blue moon indulgence, as it's heavy on all the good stuff!

1 In a large bowl, combine the beef, Worcestershire or steak sauces, finely chopped garlic, salt, and pepper. Form the mixture into twelve 1-cm thick patties.

2 Spoon 1 tablespoon of leftover macaroni and cheese in the centre of six of the patties and sprinkle with some cheese. Top each of the mac and cheese patties with one of the remaining six patties, pinch the edges together all the way around to seal the filling inside.

3 Heat the grill to medium and cook for 10–12 minutes or until desired doneness. Turn carefully halfway through. During the last 5 minutes of cooking, place the onion on top.

4 Spread the cut sides of the buns with the spicy ketchup, or your preferred sauces. Layer the lettuce, patties, pickles, and onion on the bun, top with the lid, and enjoy.

Mac & Cheese Topping

Mac and cheese is amazingly versatile. It can be served as a main course, as a side, and even used as a topping. Try it on hamburgers, hot dogs, fried chicken burgers, brisket and pulled pork sandwiches, and more. You can even top your topping – with jalapeño chillies, pickles, hot sauce, ketchup, or whatever takes your fancy.

MEXICAN STREET CORN
MAC & CHEESE

COOK TIME: 30 MINUTES
SERVES: 4–6

4 tbsp butter

450g large shells or pipe pasta, uncooked

250g grated mature Cheddar cheese

250g grated Cheddar with chilli cheese

1 bag (350g) frozen sweetcorn (or use fresh or canned)

1 litre evaporated milk

1.2 litres vegetable stock

1 tsp chilli powder

½ tsp garlic powder

Zest of 1 lime

1 tsp salt, plus extra to taste

½ tsp freshly ground black pepper

60g grated cotija or feta cheese

10g chopped coriander

This recipe is a lot of fun. It utilizes large shells and a robust combination of flavours. This mac is a nod to a favourite street-cart dish and will surely be a hit at any summer barbecue. It mixes Cheddar and Cheddar with chilli cheeses with sweetcorn, chilli powder, and a little bit of salt and lime to bring out the brightness of the cojita cheese. All in all, this dish offers a lot of flavour, texture, and colour to any table it ends up on. It also pairs very nicely with margaritas!

1 In a large saucepan, combine the butter, pasta, Cheddars, corn, evaporated milk, vegetable stock, chilli powder, garlic powder, lime zest, salt, and pepper and stir to combine. Turn the heat to medium-high and bring to a simmer, stirring every few minutes so the pasta doesn't stick to the bottom of the pan.

2 After the mixture simmers for about 1 minute, reduce the heat to low or medium–low and gently simmer for about 10 minutes, or until the pasta is al dente and the sauce is smooth and creamy. Stir every couple of minutes while it's cooking.

3 Top the mac and cheese with the cotija or feta and coriander and enjoy!

CAULIFLOWER MAC & CHEESE

COOK TIME: 1 HOUR

SERVES: 4-6

2 heads)of cauliflower, chopped into 2.5-cm pieces

115g unsalted butter, plus extra for greasing

1.2 litres whole milk

60g plain flour

2 tsp salt

¼ tsp freshly ground black pepper

¼ tsp freshly grated nutmeg

¼ tsp garlic powder

Pinch of chipotle chilli powder, or to taste (optional)

500g grated mature and/or mild Cheddar cheese

250g grated mild Cheddar cheese or 125g grated Pecorino Romano cheese

1 bag (350g) garlic butter croutons

Thyme sprigs, to garnish (optional)

While technically not a 'mac' (there's no use of a pasta), this dish is a gluten-free version of the beloved dish. Cooking the cauliflower to al dente and using it as your pasta will make you realize that there are much healthier ways to indulge in this comfort food once in a while. This is also a great way to get your daily vegetable dose! This dish makes a perfect main served alongside a crisp salad and a glass of Sauvignon Blanc.

1 Fill a microwaveable bowl with 2.5cm of water, add the cauliflower, and microwave on high for 8 minutes. Drain the cauliflower and set aside.

2 Preheat the oven to 190°C/Fan 170°C/Gas 5. Lightly butter a 3-litre casserole dish.

3 Heat the milk in a medium saucepan over a low–medium heat.

4 In a separate high-sided frying pan or large saucepan, melt the butter over a low–medium heat. When the butter bubbles, add the flour. Cook, whisking the butter and flour, for about 1 minute. Once the mixture (roux) has thickened, slowly pour in the hot milk about 60ml at a time, whisking constantly, until the mixture bubbles and becomes a thick sauce. (You may have to turn the heat down if the sauce thickens too quickly, use your best judgment.)

5 Once the sauce has thickened, remove the pan from the heat. Stir in the salt, black pepper, nutmeg, garlic powder, chipotle chilli powder, if using, and all but 115–155g Cheddar cheese (or 50g Parmesan, if using). Mix until a smooth sauce forms, then stir in the cauliflower.

6 Transfer the mixture to the baking dish.
Pulse the croutons in a food processor to
breadcrumbs. Sprinkle the remaining Cheddar
cheese and the breadcrumbs over the top.
Bake until the cheese has browned,
15–20 minutes. Cool for at
least 5 minutes, then serve
hot, garnished with fresh
thyme, if using.

Waste Not

Ideas for Leftover Mac & Cheese

TIPS FOR REVIVING LEFTOVER
MAC & CHEESE

Mac and cheese isn't always one of those things that holds up to be as amazing the second day as well as it does when it's freshly made (but if you must, add a little moisture – like milk – when you reheat it). That being said, mac and cheese leftovers can be used in a variety of ways and take second-day mac to a whole new level. Take your L.O.s up a notch by re-imagining them as burger toppings, sandwiches, breakfast cups, and much more. This section provides a range of recipes, but it's best used as inspiration to see what you can do to make mac and cheese leftovers a delicious day two meal – with no waste.

Simple Mac & Cheese Toastie

COOK TIME: 15 MINUTES

SERVES: 4

600g leftover mac and cheese or ½ Perfect Stovetop Mac & Cheese or 3-ingredient Mac & Cheese (any recipe will do, these are recommended)

8 slices sourdough or other dense bread

8 slices American or Cheddar cheese

55g butter or mayonnaise

This grilled mac and cheese sandwich combines two childhood favourites and makes a fantastic lunch or last-minute meal. Top with some tomato slices or pickles to give it extra flavour! It can also be jazzed up by pairing it with tomato soup and also a simple side salad.

1 In a small frying pan over a low–medium heat, reheat the leftover mac and cheese for 3–4 minutes. Once warm, top four slices of bread with even amounts of leftover mac, leaving a little space between the edges of the bread and the filling. Top each with a slice of cheese.

2 Butter or spread mayonnaise over the other four slices of bread and place, butter side up, on top of the mac and cheese half sandwiches. Flip with a spatula and turn the heat to medium. Toast for 1–2 minutes, then remove from the heat and transfer to a plate. Cool for a few minutes and serve hot.

Pulled Pork MC Sandwich

COOK TIME: 20 MINUTES

SERVES: 4

115g butter, plus extra for cooking

120ml mayonnaise

800g leftover mac and cheese

250ml barbecue or chimichanga sauce

400g pulled pork

8 slices buttermilk or white bread

12 slices mature Cheddar cheese

Red onions, sliced

Pickles or gherkins

BBQ Baked Beans (page 65 and coleslaw (page 64) as optional sides

Pulled pork mac + cheese sandwiches are the most delicious way to use leftovers. This giant mess of a sandwich is reminiscent of something you might find on a food truck at a street festival. The cheese, pork and barbecue sauce make a perfect flavour combination, especially on a buttermilk bun and topped with pickles and sliced red onion.

1 In a medium–large bowl, beat the butter (keeping a small pat for the skillet) and mayonnaise (you can do this by hand or using a hand-held/stand mixer). Set aside.

2 On a baking tray or in a cake tin or baking dish, spread the mac and cheese to about 2.5 cm thick. Cover and chill until the mixture is firm, about 1 hour. Once firm, cut the mac and cheese into squares, a little smaller than the bread slices you are using.

3 Combine the barbecue or chimichanga sauce and pulled pork in a saucepan over a low–medium heat and cook for about 5 minutes, or until the pulled pork is warm.

4 Melt a little butter in a frying pan over a medium heat. Spread the butter/mayo mixture on one side of each slice of bread. Flip over half of the bread slices and add a slice of Cheddar, a mac and cheese square, and another slice of Cheddar. Add the pulled pork, another slice of Cheddar, and some sliced red onions and pickles, then top with the remaining bread slices, butter/mayo side up.

5 Cook in a frying pan over a low–medium heat until the cheese melts and the bread is golden, 4–5 minutes per side.

6 Serve with baked beans and coleslaw…and more mac and cheese, if you like!

Breakfast Egg & Mac Muffins

COOKING TIME 10–15 MINUTES

MAKES 12 MUFFINS

Oil, for greasing

6–8 eggs

Salt and freshly ground black pepper (optional)

600g leftover Slow Cooker White Mac & Cheese (page 55)

115g grated cheese of your choice

These breakfast muffins can be made ahead and frozen, then quickly warmed in the morning for a quick on-the-go breakfast.

1 Preheat the oven to 180°C/Fan 160°C/Gas 4. Grease or line a 12-hole muffin tin or 6 large muffin tins with paper cupcake/muffin cases.

2 Beat the eggs in a bowl and add salt and pepper, if you like. Set aside.

3 Fill the holes in the muffin tins two-thirds of the way with leftover mac and cheese. Pour the beaten eggs on top, then sprinkle each muffin cup with an equal amount of cheese. Bake for 10–15 minutes until the eggs are set. Cool for a few minutes, then pop out or loosen the edges and release. Serve warm.

Mac & Cheese Bacon Cups

COOK TIME: 20 MINUTES
MAKES: 12 BACON CUPS

450g sliced bacon
600g leftover mac and cheese
Salt and freshly ground black pepper, to taste
30g grated Cheddar cheese
Chopped fresh chives, to serve (optional)

This bacon cup recipe can be used as an edible bowl for just about any leftover mac and cheese recipe in this book. They can also be filled with an egg and topped with mac and cheese (or just plain cheese for a simpler version, if you like) for a breakfast egg cup.

1 Preheat the oven to 200°C/Fan 180°C/Gas 6.

2 Place the slices of bacon in the holes of 12-hole muffin tin, wrapping around the inside of the tin in a circle. Place in the oven on a baking tray and bake the bacon for 10 minutes.

3 Remove the bacon from the oven and pour out any excess grease. Using a spoon, fill the cups with leftover mac and cheese. Sprinkle with salt, pepper (if needed), and the Cheddar cheese. Bake for another 10 minutes, or until the cheese on top melts and is golden brown. Cool for about 5 minutes.

4 Run a knife around the edge of each cup to loosen and remove. Sprinkle with chives, if you like.

Index

A

almond milk: Vegan Mac
& Cheese 37
American cheese:
Cheese Lover's
5-cheese Mac 52-3
Chicken Pot Pie Mac &
Cheese 105
Jalapeño Pepper Mac
& Cheese 80-1
Monticello Mac &
Cheese 73
Philly (Mac &) Cheese
Steak 101
Simple Mac & Cheese
Toastie 150
Stuffed Mac & Cheese
108-9
andouille sausage:
Cajun Mac & Cheese
66-7
artichokes: Spinach &
Artichoke Dip Mac &
Cheese 42-3

B

Bacon: 4-alarm Mac &
Cheese 40-1
Bacon & Blue Cheese
Mac 98-9
Deep-fried Mac &
Cheese Bites 10-11
Mac & Carbonara
82-3
Mac & Cheese Bacon
Cups 155
Meat Lover's Mac &
Cheese 111-13
Skillet Bacon
Primavera Mac &
Cheese 126-7
Baked Beans, BBQ 65

Baked Mac & Cheese,
Perfect 30-1
Baked Mac & Cheese
Bites 19
Baked Mac & Cheese
Pizza Crust 45
basil: Mozzarella Mac
& Cheese (Caprese)
78-9
Homemade Pesto 87
BBQ sauce: BBQ Baked
Beans 65
Slow Cooker Pulled
Pork Mac & Cheese
59-61
beef: BBQ Baked Beans
65
Chili Mac & Cheese 77
Lasagne Mac 69
Mac & Cheese Brisket
Bites 15-17
Mac & Cheese Stuffed
Burgers 140
Philly (Mac &) Cheese
Steak 101
Skillet Cheeseburger
Mac 88
Taco Mac & Cheese
46
Blue cheese: Bacon &
Blue Cheese Mac &
Cheese 98-9
Monticello Mac &
Cheese 73
bratwurst: Oktoberfest
Mac & Cheese 128-9
bread: Easy Sourdough
119
French Onion Mac &
Cheese Soup 20
Mac & Cheese Burger
Buns 139

Pulled Pork MC
Sandwich 153
Simple Mac & Cheese
Toastie 150
Breakfast Egg & Mac
Muffins 154
Breakfast Mac &
Cheese 133-4
brioche: Mac & Cheese
Stuffed Burgers 140
Broccoli: Slow Cooker
Broccoli-Cheddar Mac
& Cheese 56
Buffalo Sauce 125
Buffalo Chicken Mac
& Cheese 123-4
Burger Buns, Mac &
Cheese 139
Burgers: Mac & Cheese
Stuffed Burgers 140
Mac My Burger 138-41
Buttermilk & Sourdough
Mac & Cheese
117-18

C

cabbage: Coleslaw 64
Cajun Mac & Cheese
66-7
camembert: Monticello
Mac & Cheese 73
carrots: Chicken Pot Pie
Mac & Cheese 105
Coleslaw 64
cashews: Vegan Mac &
Cheese 37
Cauliflower Mac &
Cheese 144-5
celery: Chicken Pot Pie
Mac & Cheese 105
Monticello Mac &
Cheese 73

Cheddar: 3-ingredient
Mac & Cheese 38
4-alarm Mac & Cheese
40-1
Breakfast Mac &
Cheese 133-4
Buffalo Chicken Mac &
Cheese 123-4
Buttermilk &
Sourdough Mac &
Cheese 117-18
Cajun Mac & Cheese
66-7
Cauliflower Mac &
Cheese 144-5
Cheese Lover's
5-cheese Mac 52-3
Chicken Pot Pie Mac &
Cheese 105
Chili Mac & Cheese 77
Family Stovetop Mac
& Cheese 34
Fancy Mac & Cheese
91-2
Jalapeño Pepper Mac
& Cheese 80-1
Mac & Carbonara
82-3
Mac & Cheese Bacon
Cups 155
Mac & Cheese Muffins
23-5
Mac & Cheese in a
Mug 27
Mac & Cheese Waffles
135-7
Meat Lover's Mac &
Cheese 111-13
Mexican Street Corn
Mac & Cheese 142
Monticello Mac &
Cheese 73

Oktoberfest Mac &
Cheese 128–9
Perfect Baked Mac &
Cheese 30–1
Philly (Mac &) Cheese
Steak 101
Pizza Mac Bake 120
Pulled Pork MC
Sandwich 153
Pumpkin Mac &
Cheese 97
Simple Mac & Cheese
Toastie 150
Skillet Bacon
Primavera Mac &
Cheese 126–7
Skillet Cheeseburger
Mac & Cheese
88
Slow Cooker Broccoli-
Cheddar Mac &
Cheese 56
Slow Cooker Pulled
Pork Mac & Cheese
59–61
Slow Cooker White
Cheddar Mac &
Cheese 55
Southern Mac &
Cheese 49
Stuffed Mac & Cheese
108–9
Taco Mac & Cheese
46
Truffle Mac & Cheese
74–5
Vegas-style Mac &
Cheese 102–3
Cheese Lover's
5-cheese Mac 52–3
Cheeseburger Mac &
Cheese, Skillet 88

Chicken: Buffalo
Chicken Mac &
Cheese 123–4
Chicken Parmesan
Mac 70
Chicken Pot Pie Mac &
Cheese 105
Chili Mac & Cheese 77
Coleslaw 64
corn: Mexican Street
Corn Mac & Cheese
142
cotija cheese: Mexican
Street Corn Mac &
Cheese 142
crackers: Chicken Pot
Pie Mac & Cheese 105
Stuffed Mac & Cheese
108–9
cream: Jalapeño Pepper
Mac & Cheese 80–1
Stuffed Mac & Cheese
108–9
cream cheese: Buffalo
Chicken Mac &
Cheese 123–4
Jalapeño Pepper Mac
& Cheese 80–1
Philly (Mac &) Cheese
Steak 101
Slow Cooker Broccoli-
Cheddar Mac &
Cheese 56
Slow Cooker White
Cheddar Mac &
Cheese 55
Stuffed Mac & Cheese
108–9
Vegas-style Mac &
Cheese 102–3
croutons: 4-alarm Mac
& Cheese 40–1

Bacon & Blue Cheese
Mac & Cheese
98–9
Buttermilk &
Sourdough Mac &
Cheese 117–18
Cauliflower Mac &
Cheese 144–5
Deep-fried Mac &
Cheese Bites 10–11
Fancy Mac & Cheese
91–2
Lobster Mac & Cheese
93–5
Mac & Cheese Brisket
Bites 15–17
Mac & Cheese Muffins
23–5
Perfect Baked Mac &
Cheese 30–1
Truffle Mac & Cheese
74–5

D
Deep-fried Mac &
Cheese Bites 10–11

E
eggs: Breakfast Egg &
Mac Muffins 154
Mac & Cheese Burger
Buns 139
Emmental: Monticello
Mac & Cheese 73
evaporated milk:
3-ingredient Mac &
Cheese 38
Cheese Lover's
5-cheese Mac 52–3
Mexican Street Corn
Mac & Cheese 142
Pizza Mac Bake 120

Southern Mac &
Cheese 49

F
Family Stovetop Mac &
Cheese 34
Fancy Mac & Cheese
91–2
feta cheese: Mexican
Street Corn Mac &
Cheese 142
Fontina: 4-alarm Mac &
Cheese 40–1
Fancy Mac & Cheese
91–2
Spinach & Artichoke
Dip Mac & Cheese
42–3
French Onion Mac &
Cheese Soup 20–1

G
garlic butter croutons:
4-alarm Mac & Cheese
40–1
Bacon & Blue Cheese
Mac & Cheese 98–9
Buttermilk &
Sourdough Mac &
Cheese 117–18
Cauliflower Mac &
Cheese 144–5
Fancy Mac & Cheese
91–2
Lobster Mac & Cheese
93–5
Mac & Cheese Muffins
23–5
Meat Lover's Mac &
Cheese 111–13
Perfect Baked Mac &
Cheese 30–1

Truffle Mac & Cheese 74–5
Wild Mushroom Mac & Cheese 106–7
goat's cheese: Spinach & Artichoke Dip Mac & Cheese 42–3
Gouda: 4-alarm Mac & Cheese 40–1
Breakfast Mac & Cheese 133–4
Cheese Lover's 5-Cheese Mac 52–3
Pumpkin Mac & Cheese 97
Southern Mac & Cheese 49
Sriracha & Shrimp Mac & Cheese 115–16
Gruyère: Cheese Lover's 5-cheese Mac 52–3
Fancy Mac & Cheese 91–2
Lobster Mac & Cheese 93–5
Monticello Mac & Cheese 73
Mozzarella Mac & Cheese (Caprese) 78–9
Truffle Mac & Cheese 74–5
Wild Mushroom Mac & Cheese 106–7

H
Havarti cheese: Pesto Mac & Cheese 85
Sriracha & Shrimp Mac & Cheese 115–16
hot pepper sauce: Buffalo Sauce 125

I
Italian sausage: Baked Mac & Cheese Pizza Crust 45

J
jalapeños: 4-alarm Mac & Cheese 40–1
Breakfast Mac & Cheese 133–4
Jalapeño Pepper Mac & Cheese 80–1

L
lager beer: Oktoberfest Mac & Cheese 128–9
Lasagne Mac & Cheese 69
lettuce: Taco Mac & Cheese 46
Lobster Mac & Cheese 93–5

M
Mac & Carbonara 82–3
mac and cheese bites:
Baked Mac & Cheese Bites 19
Deep-fried Mac & Cheese Bites 10–11
Mac & Cheese Brisket Bites 15–17
Mac My Burger 138–41
Manchego: Monticello Mac & Cheese 73
Meat Lover's Mac & Cheese 111–13
Mexican Street Corn Mac & Cheese 142
Monticello Mac & Cheese 73
mozzarella: Baked Mac & Cheese Pizza Crust

45
Jalapeño Pepper Mac & Cheese 80–1
Lasagne Mac & Cheese 69
Monticello Mac & Cheese 73
Mozzarella Mac & Cheese (Caprese) 78–9
Pesto Mac & Cheese 85
Slow Cooker Broccoli-Cheddar Mac & Cheese 56
Slow Cooker White Cheddar Mac & Cheese 55
Spinach & Artichoke Dip Mac & Cheese 42–3
Mozzarella Mac & Cheese (Caprese) 78–9
Chicken Parmesan Mac 70
Muffins: Breakfast Egg & Mac Muffins 154
Mac & Cheese Muffins 23–5
Mug, Mac & Cheese in a 27
mushrooms: Monticello Mac & Cheese 73
Wild Mushroom Mac & Cheese 106–7

N
nutritional yeast: Vegan Mac & Cheese 37

O
Oktoberfest Mac &

Cheese 128–9
onions: French Onion Mac & Cheese Soup 20–1

P
Panko breadcrumbs:
Deep-fried Mac & Cheese Bites 10–11
Mac & Cheese Brisket Bites 15–17
Vegan Mac & Cheese 37
Parmesan: Baked Mac & Cheese Pizza Crust 45
Chicken Parmesan Mac & Cheese 70
Homemade Pesto 87
Mac & Carbonara 82–3
Slow Cooker Broccoli-Cheddar Mac & Cheese 56
Slow Cooker White Cheddar Mac & Cheese 55
Vegas-style Mac & Cheese 102–3
peas: Chicken Pot Pie Mac & Cheese 105
Pecorino Romano:
Breakfast Mac & Cheese 133–4
Family Stovetop Mac & Cheese 34
Homemade Pesto 87
Lobster Mac & Cheese 93–5
Mac & Cheese Muffins 23–5
Mac & Cheese Waffles 135–7
Perfect Baked Mac & Cheese 30–1

Pesto Mac & Cheese
85
Spinach & Artichoke
Dip Mac & Cheese
42–3
Wild Mushroom Mac &
Cheese 106–7
Pepperoni: Baked Mac &
Cheese Pizza Crust 45
Pizza Mac Bake 120
Peppers: BBQ Baked
Beans 65
Breakfast Mac &
Cheese 133–4
Cajun Mac & Cheese
66–7
Chili Mac & Cheese 77
Philly (Mac &) Cheese
Steak 101
Pizza Mac Bake 120
Perfect Baked Mac &
Cheese 30–1
Pesto: Homemade
Pesto 87
Pesto Mac & Cheese
85
Philly (Mac &) Cheese
Steak 101
pine nuts: Homemade
Pesto 87
Pizza sauce: Baked Mac
& Cheese Pizza Crust
45
Pizza Mac Bake 120
Pork: Pulled Pork MC
Sandwich 153
Slow Cooker Pulled
Pork Mac & Cheese
59–61
provolone: Philly (Mac &)
Cheese Steak 101
Pulled Pork MC
Sandwich 153

Pumpkin Mac & Cheese
97

R
Red Leicester: Cheese
Lover's 5-cheese Mac
52–3
Southern Mac &
Cheese 49
red kidney beans: Chili
Mac & Cheese 77
Roquefort: Monticello
Mac & Cheese 73

S
salads: Coleslaw 64
Sandwich, Pulled Pork
MC 153
sausages: Baked Mac
& Cheese Pizza Crust
45
Breakfast Mac &
Cheese 133–4
Cajun Mac & Cheese
66–7
Meat Lover's Mac &
Cheese 111–13
shallots: Wild Mushroom
Mac & Cheese 106–7
Shrimps: Sriracha &
Shrimp Mac & Cheese
115–16
Skillet Bacon Primavera
Mac & Cheese 126–7
Skillet Cheeseburger
Mac & Cheese 88
Slow Cooker Broccoli-
Cheddar Mac &
Cheese 56
Slow Cooker Pulled Pork
Mac & Cheese 59–61
Slow Cooker White
Cheddar Mac &

Cheese 55
sodium citrate 7
Soup, French Onion Mac
& Cheese 20–1
sour cream: Skillet
Bacon Primavera Mac
& Cheese 126–7
Southern Mac &
Cheese 49
Taco Mac & Cheese 46
Sourdough: Buttermilk
& Sourdough Mac &
Cheese 117–18
Easy Sourdough 119
Simple Mac & Cheese
Toastie 150
Southern Mac & Cheese
49
Spinach: Skillet Bacon
Primavera Mac &
Cheese 126–7
Spinach & Artichoke
Dip Mac & Cheese
42–3
squash: Skillet Bacon
Primavera Mac &
Cheese 126–7
Sriracha & Shrimp Mac
& Cheese 115–16
Stovetop Mac &
Cheese, Family 34
Stuffed Mac & Cheese
108–9

T
Taco Seasoning 48
Taco Mac & Cheese 46
tater tots: Breakfast
Mac & Cheese 133–4
Texas BBQ Buffet 62–5
3-ingredient Mac &
Cheese 38
Baked Mac & Cheese

Pizza Crust 45
Lasagne Mac &
Cheese 69
Taco Mac & Cheese 46
Toastie, Simple Mac &
Cheese 150
tomato sauce: Chicken
Parmesan Mac 70
Lasagne Mac &
Cheese 69
Skillet Cheeseburger
Mac & Cheese 88
tomatoes: Chili Mac &
Cheese 77
Mozzarella Mac &
Cheese (Caprese)
78–9
Pizza Mac Bake 120
Skillet Bacon
Primavera Mac &
Cheese 126–7
Taco Mac & Cheese 46
Topping, Mac & Cheese
141
Truffle Mac & Cheese
74–5

V
Vegan Mac & Cheese 37
Vegas-style Mac &
Cheese 102–3

W
Waffles, Mac & Cheese
135–7
Wild Mushroom Mac &
Cheese 106–7

Acknowledgments

The 'author' of any book is really just the name on the cover. With a book like *Mac & Cheese*, this was a collaborative journey. This book was made thanks to a collection of extremely talented human beings. I would like to thank Caitlin Doyle for having an amazing vision. I feel extremely privileged to be able to help bring this book to life. I'd also like to thank our FABULOUS Designer, Sophie Yamamoto of maru studio; our AMAZING copyeditor, Helena Caldon; the BEAUTIFUL picture research by Caitlin Doyle and Shifting Pixels; and our proofreaders Kathy Steer and Rachel Malig and indexer Vanessa Bird, plus mac and cheese experts Steve King and Saoirse Doyle Fardell.

Working with HarperCollins UK is a privilege for me and I am honoured to be among many talented and innovative writers.

Lastly, I'd like to thank my fella Jeremy, my friends Brittany and Eric, my students and friends at Hawthorne Scholastic Academy (Go Hurricanes!), and my entire family for always buying my books, making the recipes/testing, and for always giving love, support, and amazing feedback.

Picture credits

All reasonable efforts have been made by the authors and publishers to trace the copyright owners of the material quoted in this book and of any images reproduced in this book. In the event that the authors or publishers are notified of any mistakes or omissions by copyright owners after publication, the authors and publishers will endeavour to rectify the position accordingly for any subsequent printing.

All listed in alphabetical order

Cover: front cover: YesPhotographers/Shutterstock.com; back cover: Elena Veselova/Shutterstock.com (top); Ivan Dziuba/Shutterstock.com (middle); Alp Aksoy/Shutterstock.com (bottom)

Alexander Prokopenko/Shutterstock.com: 83; AlexPro9500/GettyImages.co.uk: 54; Ali Jenkins/Shutterstock.com: 58; Alp Aksoy/Shutterstock.com: 14, 17; AS Foodstudio/Shutterstock.com: 50; Bartosz Luczak/Shutterstock.com: 89; bonchan/Shutterstock.com: 114; Brent Hofacker/Shutterstock.com: 12, 44, 47, 61, 65, 125; Carey Jaman/Shutterstock.com: 21; Charles Brutlag/Shutterstock.com: 76; Cheyne Kobzoff/Shutterstock.com: 90; Chudo2307/Shutterstock.com: 26; DronG/Shutterstock.com: 18; Elena Shashkina/Shutterstock.com: 43, 67, 96, 145; Elena Veselova/Shutterstock.com: 22, 25, 53; Ezume Images/Shutterstock.com: 39, 100; Foodio/Shutterstock.com: 95; gowithstock/Shutterstock.com: 143; Graficam Ahmed Saeed/Shutterstock.com: 71; Hashem Issam Alshanableh/Shutterstock.com: 138; Ika Rahma H/Shutterstock.com: 104; Irina Rostokina/Shutterstock.com: 72; iuliia_n/Shutterstock.com: 154; Ivan Danik/Shutterstock.com: 126; Ivan Dziuba/Shutterstock.com: 32; joshuaraineyphotography/GettyImages.co.uk: 132; Joshua Resnick/Shutterstock.com: 63; Joyce Mar/Shutterstock.com: 75; Julia Mikhaylova/Shutterstock.com: 121; Kathy Byrd/GettyImages.co.uk: 129; Laura Sullivan12/Shutterstock.com: 36; LauriPatterson/GettyImages.co.uk: 137, 151; Liliya Kandrashevich/Shutterstock.com: 57; Lynne Mitchell/GettyImages.co.uk: 35; mahirart/Shutterstock.com: 119, manyakotic/GettyImages.co.uk: 110; MariaKovaleva/Shutterstock.com: 68, 87, 99; Marie Sonmez Photography/Shutterstock.com: 113, 118, 138; Martha Graham/Shutterstock.com: 152; Meal Prep on Fleek/Shutterstock.com: 122; nesavinov/Shutterstock.com: 64; Parintorn Chungpradit/Shutterstock.com: 155; Sunvic/Shutterstock.com: 84; Tatiana Vorona/Shutterstock.com: 79; The Image Party/Shutterstock.com: 40; The Influence Agency TIA/Shutterstock.com: 141; Toasted Pictures/Shutterstock.com: 48; ungvar/Shutterstock.com: 108; Vladimir Mironov /GettyImages.co.uk: 103; vm2002/Shutterstock.com: 80; wsmahar/GettyImages.co.uk: 107